HENRY V

William Shakespeare

D0107166

This edition published by Spark Publishing

Spark Publishing
A Division of SparkNotes LLC
120 Fifth Avenue, 8th Floor
New York, NY 10011

Please submit all comments and questions or report errors to www.sparknotes.com/errors

Printed and bound in the United States

ISBN 1-58663-520-4

A Prologue from the Bard

Brave scholars, blessed with time and energy,
    At school, fair Harvard, set about to glean,
From dusty tomes and modern poetry,
    All truths and knowledge formerly unseen.
From forth the hungry minds of these good folk
    Study guides, star-floss'd, soon came to life;
Whose deep and deft analysis awoke
    The latent "A"s of those in lit'rary strife.
Aim far past passing—insight from our trove
    Will free your comprehension from its cage.
Our SparkNotes' worth, online we also prove;
    Behold this book! Same brains, but paper page.
If patient or "whatever," please attend,
    What you have missed, our toil shall strive to mend.

CONTENTS

CONTEXT

THE MOST INFLUENTIAL WRITER in all of English literature, William Shakespeare was born in 1564 to a successful middle-class glove-maker in Stratford-upon-Avon, England. Shakespeare attended grammar school, but his formal education proceeded no further. In 1582 he married an older woman, Anne Hathaway, and had three children with her. Around 1590 he left his family behind and traveled to London to work as an actor and playwright. Public and critical acclaim quickly followed, and Shakespeare eventually became the most popular playwright in England and part-owner of the Globe Theater. His career bridged the reigns of Elizabeth I (ruled 1558–1603) and James I (ruled 1603–1625), and he was a favorite of both monarchs. Indeed, James granted Shakespeare's company the greatest possible compliment by bestowing upon its members the title of King's Men. Wealthy and renowned, Shakespeare retired to Stratford and died in 1616 at the age of fifty-two. At the time of Shakespeare's death, literary luminaries such as Ben Jonson hailed his works as timeless.

Shakespeare's works were collected and printed in various editions during the century following his death, and by the early eighteenth century, his reputation as the greatest poet ever to write in English was well established. The unprecedented admiration garnered by his works led to a fierce curiosity about Shakespeare's life, but the dearth of biographical information has left many details of Shakespeare's personal history shrouded in mystery. Some people have concluded from this fact and from Shakespeare's modest education that Shakespeare's plays were actually written by someone else—Francis Bacon and the Earl of Oxford are the two most popular candidates—but the support for this claim is overwhelmingly circumstantial, and the theory is not taken seriously by many scholars.

In the absence of credible evidence to the contrary, Shakespeare must be viewed as the author of the thirty-seven plays and 154 sonnets that bear his name. The legacy of this body of work is immense. A number of Shakespeare's plays seem to have transcended even the category of brilliance, becoming so influential as to affect profoundly the course of Western literature and culture ever after.

CONTEXT

Henry V is one of Shakespeare's so-called history plays. It forms the fourth part of a tetralogy (a four-part series) dealing with the historical rise of the English royal House of Lancaster. (The three plays that come before it are *Richard II, I Henry IV,* and *II Henry IV.*) *Henry V*, probably written in 1599, is one of the most popular of Shakespeare's history plays. It contains a host of entertaining characters who speak in many accents and languages. The play is full of noble speeches, heroic battles, and valiant English underdogs who fight their way to victory against all odds. Additionally, King Henry seems to be a perfect leader—brave, modest, and fiercely focused, but with a sense of humor to match.

The play's treatment of King Henry V, however, is more problematic than it seems at first glance. Henry is a model of traditional heroism, but his value system is confusing. After all, his sense of honor leads him to invade a nonaggressive country and to slaughter thousands of people. He sentences to death former friends and prisoners of war while claiming to value mercy, and he never acknowledges that he bears any responsibility for the bloodshed he has initiated. It is useful to read the play with an eye toward these discrepancies, which Shakespeare examines in a complicated exploration of the nature of kingship. Whether or not he appears to be an admirable man, Henry is presented as a nearly ideal king, with a diamond-hard focus, an intractable resolve, and the willpower to subordinate his own personal feelings to the needs of his nation and his throne. The brilliance of Henry's speeches and his careful cultivation of his image make him an effective and inspiring leader. Whether he emerges from the play as a heroic figure or merely a king as cold as he is brilliant depends largely on each individual reader's interpretation.

Plot Overview

THE PLAY IS SET IN ENGLAND in the early fifteenth century. The political situation in England is tense: King Henry IV has died, and his son, the young King Henry V, has just assumed the throne. Several bitter civil wars have left the people of England restless and dissatisfied. Furthermore, in order to gain the respect of the English people and the court, Henry must live down his wild adolescent past, when he used to consort with thieves and drunkards at the Boar's Head Tavern on the seedy side of London.

Henry lays claim to certain parts of France, based on his distant roots in the French royal family and on a very technical interpretation of ancient land laws. When the young prince, or Dauphin, of France sends Henry an insulting message in response to these claims, Henry decides to invade France. Supported by the English noblemen and clergy, Henry gathers his troops for war.

Henry's decision to invade France trickles down to affect the common people he rules. In the Boar's Head Tavern in Eastcheap, some of the king's former friends—whom he rejected when he rose to the throne—prepare to leave their homes and families. Bardolph, Pistol, and Nim are common lowlifes and part-time criminals, on the opposite end of the social spectrum from their royal former companion. As they prepare for the war, they remark on the death of Falstaff, an elderly knight who was once King Henry's closest friend.

Just before his fleet sets sail, King Henry learns of a conspiracy against his life. The three traitors working for the French beg for mercy, but Henry denies their request. He orders that the trio, which includes a former friend named Scrope, be executed. The English sail for France, where they fight their way across the country. Against incredible odds, they continue to win after conquering the town of Harfleur, where Henry gives an impassioned speech to motivate his soldiers to victory. Among the officers in King Henry's army are men from all parts of Britain, such as Fluellen, a Welsh captain. As the English advance, Nim and Bardolph are caught looting and are hanged at King Henry's command.

The climax of the war comes at the famous Battle of Agincourt, at which the English are outnumbered by the French five to one. The night before the battle, King Henry disguises himself as a common soldier and talks to many of the soldiers in his camp, learning who they are and what they think of the great battle in which they have been swept up. When he is by himself, he laments his ever-present responsibilities as king. In the morning, he prays to God and gives a powerful, inspiring speech to his soldiers. Miraculously, the English win the battle, and the proud French must surrender at last. Some time later, peace negotiations are finally worked out: Henry will marry Catherine, the daughter of the French king. Henry's son will be the king of France, and the marriage will unite the two kingdoms.

CHARACTER LIST

Like most of Shakespeare's plays, Henry V exists in two different early printed versions: the Folio version of 1623 and an earlier Quarto version. There are many differences between the two versions, the most important of which involve the assignment of the speeches of Westmorland, Warwick, the Dauphin, and Bourbon. Additionally, the character called Clarence in the Quarto is called Bedford in the Folio.

King Henry V The young, recently crowned king of England. Henry is brilliant, focused, fearless, and committed to the responsibilities of kingship. These responsibilities often force him to place his personal feelings second to the needs of the crown. Henry is a brilliant orator who uses his skill to justify his claims and to motivate his troops. Once Henry has resolved to conquer France, he pursues his goal relentlessly to the end.

Chorus A single character who introduces each of the play's five acts. Like the group of singers who comprised the chorus in Greek drama, the Chorus in Henry V functions as a narrator offering commentary on the play's plot and themes.

The Dukes of Exeter, Westmorland, Salisbury, and Warwick Trusted advisors to King Henry and the leaders of his military. The Duke of Exeter, who is also Henry's uncle, is entrusted with carrying important messages to the French king.

The Dukes of Clarence, Bedford, and Gloucester Henry's three younger brothers. Clarence, Bedford, and Gloucester are noblemen and fighters.

The Archbishop of Canterbury and the Bishop of Ely Wealthy and powerful English clergymen. The Archbishop of Canterbury and the Bishop of Ely do not go to fight in the war, but their urging and fund-raising are important factors in Henry's initial decision to invade France.

Cambridge, Scrope, and Grey Three conspirators against King Henry. Cambridge, Scrope, and Grey are bribed by French agents to kill Henry before he sets sail for France. Scrope's betrayal of his king is particularly surprising, as Scrope and Henry are good friends.

York and Suffolk Two noble cousins who die together at the Battle of Agincourt.

The King of France Charles VI. A capable leader, Charles does not underestimate King Henry, as his son, the Dauphin, does.

Isabel The queen of France, married to Charles VI. Isabel does not appear until the final scene (V.ii), in which her daughter, Catherine, is betrothed to King Henry.

The Dauphin The son of the king of France and heir to the throne (until Henry takes this privilege from him). The Dauphin is a headstrong and overconfident young man, more inclined to mock the English than to make preparations to fight them. He also mocks Henry, making frequent mention of the king's irresponsible youth.

Catherine The daughter of the king of France. Catherine is eventually married off to King Henry in order to cement the peace between England and France. She speaks little English.

French noblemen and military leaders The Constable of France, the Duke of Orléans, the Duke of Britain, the Duke of Bourbon, the Earl of Grandpré, Lord Rambures, the Duke of Burgundy, and the Governor of Harfleur are

French noblemen and military leaders. Most of them are killed or captured by the English at the Battle of Agincourt, though the Duke of Burgundy survives to help with the peace negotiations between France and England. Like the Dauphin, most of these leaders are more interested in making jokes about the English than in taking them seriously as a fighting force, a tendency that leads to the eventual French defeat at Agincourt.

Sir Thomas Erpingham A wise, aged veteran of many wars who serves with Henry's campaign.

Captain Gower An army captain and a capable fighter who serves with Henry's campaign.

Captain Fluellen, Captain MacMorris, and Captain Jamy The captains of King Henry's troops from Wales, Ireland, and Scotland, respectively, all of whom have heavy accents reflecting their countries of origin. Fluellen, a close friend of Captain Gower, is the most prominent of the three. His wordiness provides comic relief, but he is also very likable and is an intelligent leader and strategist.

Ancient Pistol A commoner from London who serves in the war with Henry, and a friend of Nim and Bardolph. Pistol speaks with a blustery and melodramatic poetic diction; he is married to the hostess of the Boar's Head Tavern in London.

Bardolph A commoner from London who serves in the war with Henry, and a friend of Pistol and Nim. Bardolph is a former friend of King Henry from his wild youth. A thief and a coward, Bardolph is hanged in France for looting from the conquered towns in violation of the king's order.

Nim A commoner from London who serves in the war with Henry, and a friend of Pistol and Bardolph. Like Bardolph, Nim is hanged in France for looting from the conquered towns.

Boy   Formerly in the service of Falstaff, the nameless boy leaves London after his master's death and goes with Pistol, Nim, and Bardolph to the war in France. The boy is somewhat touchy and embarrassed that his companions are cowardly thieves.

Michael Williams, John Bates, and Alexander Court Common soldiers with whom King Henry, disguised, argues the night before the Battle of Agincourt. Though he argues heatedly with Williams, Henry is generally impressed with these men's intelligence and courage.

Hostess   The keeper of the Boar's Head Tavern in London. Mistress Quickly, as she is also known, is married to Pistol. We hear news of her death from venereal disease in Act V, scene i.

Sir John Falstaff The closest friend and mentor of the young Henry, back in his wild days. Falstaff doesn't actually appear in Henry V, but he is a major figure in the Henry IV plays. He is a jovial and frequently drunken old knight, but his heart is broken when Henry breaks his ties with him after becoming king. We hear news of Falstaff's offstage death in Act II, scenes i and iii.

Alice   The maid of the French princess Catherine. Alice has spent time in England and teaches Catherine some English, though not very well.

Montjoy   The French herald, or messenger.

Monsieur le Fer A French soldier and gentleman who is captured by Pistol at the Battle of Agincourt.

ANALYSIS OF MAJOR CHARACTERS

KING HENRY V

Though a substantial number of scenes focus on other characters, Henry directly initiates nearly all of the significant action in the play, and he is without question the play's protagonist and hero. Henry is an extraordinary figure who possesses a degree of intelligence and charisma only briefly glimpsed in Shakespeare's two *Henry IV* plays. There Henry V appears as a pleasure-seeking teenage prince who wrestles with his role as an heir to the throne.

Perhaps Henry V's most remarkable quality is his resolve: once he has set his mind to accomplishing a goal, he uses every resource at his disposal to see that it is accomplished. He carefully presents himself as an unstoppable force to whom others must actively choose how to react. This tactic may seem morally questionable, but it is a valuable psychological weapon that Henry uses to pressure his enemies into doing what he wants. Again and again, Henry acts in a manner that would be deplorable for a common citizen but that makes him an exemplary king. For example, Henry often draws criticism from modern readers for refusing to take responsibility for the war in France. He even tells the French governor at Harfleur that if the French do not surrender, they will be responsible for the carnage that Henry will create.

Another extraordinary quality Henry possesses is his facility with language. Henry's rhetorical skill is a forceful weapon, the strength of which nearly equals that of his army's swords. With words, Henry can inspire and rouse his followers, intimidate his enemies, and persuade nearly anyone who hears him. With Henry's speeches, Shakespeare creates a rhetoric that is, like Henry himself, at once candidly frank and extremely sophisticated. Henry can be cold and menacing, as when he speaks to the Dauphin's messenger; he can be passionate and uplifting, as in his St. Crispin's Day speech; and he can be gruesomely terrifying, as in his diatribe against the Governor of Harfleur. In each case, Henry's words suggest that he is merely speaking his mind at the moment, but these speeches are brilliantly crafted and work powerfully on the minds of his listeners. Henry has a very special quality for a king: the ability to present himself honestly while still manipulating his audience.

Shakespeare does not comment explicitly on Henry's motives for invading France, but it seems clear from his speeches about the weight of his responsibility that Henry is not motivated exclusively by a lust for power or land. Henry clearly takes the mantle of kingship very seriously, and he is dedicated to fulfilling the obligations of his exalted rank. He mourns his inability to sleep the untroubled sleep of the common man, hardly the behavior of a man dedicated to the pleasures of power. It also seems clear from Henry's undeniably uplifting speeches that Shakespeare intends for us to see Henry as a hero, or, at the very least, as an estimable king. Insofar as Henry is a hero, he is made so by his commitment to his responsibilities above his own personal feelings. Along with his faculty of resolve, this commitment makes him the king he is; though it sometimes causes him to make questionable personal decisions, it also helps to mitigate the effect of those decisions in our eyes.

CATHERINE

The young, pretty princess of France does not play a very active role in the progress of the narrative, but she is nevertheless significant because she typifies the role played by women in this extremely masculine play. The scenes that center on Catherine and her tutor, Alice, depict a female world that contrasts starkly with the grim, violent world in which the play's men exist. While the men fight pitched battles, yoking the course of history to the course of their bloody conflicts, Catherine lives in a much gentler and quieter milieu, generally ignorant of the larger struggle going on around her. She fills her days mainly with laughing and teasing Alice as the latter attempts to teach her English.

The fact that Catherine's scenes are in a different language from the rest of the play's scenes dramatically underscores the difference between her lifestyle and that of the men: where the soldiers speak a hard, rhythmic English, Catherine speaks in a soft, lilting French. These differences point to the fact that, while Catherine's life may be more pleasant than that of the men, the scope of her existence is extremely limited and has been chosen for her: she has become beautiful, pleasant, and yielding because she has been raised to become whatever will make her desirable to a future husband.

CHARACTER ANALYSIS

These qualities have been determined by the masculine value system around which her culture is structured.

Catherine's father hopes to marry her to a powerful leader in order to win a powerful ally, and thus Catherine has been molded into the graceful and charming woman that a powerful leader is likely to want. Shakespeare uses Catherine's English lessons with Alice to highlight her role as a tool of negotiation among the men. As the English conquer more and more of France, Catherine's potential husband seems likely to be English. Catherine thus begins to study English—not because she herself desires to speak the language (we are given almost no insight into what Catherine herself might desire), but because her father intends to marry her to his enemy in order to end the war and preserve his power in France.

FLUELLEN

Fluellen, along with Jamy and MacMorris, is one of the three foreign captains in the play. These three characters broadly represent their respective nationalities—Fluellen, for instance, is a Welshman, included in part to represent Wales in the play's exploration of the peoples of Britain. As a result, Fluellen embodies many of the comical stereotypes associated with the Welsh in Shakespeare's day: he is wordy, overly serious, and possessed of a ludicrous pseudo-Welsh accent that principally involves replacing the letter "b" with the letter "p."

However, Shakespeare also makes Fluellen a well-defined and likable individual who tends to work against the limitations of his stereotype. Though he is clownish in his early scenes, he is also extremely well informed and appears to be quite competent, especially compared to the cowardly lot of commoners from England whom he orders into battle at Harfleur. Like Bottom in *A Midsummer Night's Dream* or Falstaff in the *Henry IV* plays, Fluellen tends to steal the scenes he is in and to win the affection of his audience. The fact that Shakespeare wrote such a role for a Welsh character is a strong sign that Fluellen is intended as far more than a comic compendium of ethnic stereotypes.

THEMES, MOTIFS & SYMBOLS

THEMES

Themes are the fundamental and often universal ideas explored in a literary work.

THE RUTHLESSNESS OF THE GOOD KING

In presenting the figure of its heroic yet ruthless protagonist, *Henry V*'s predominant concern is the nature of leadership and its relationship to morality. The play proposes that the qualities that define a good ruler are not necessarily the same qualities that define a good person. Henry is an extraordinarily good leader: he is intelligent, focused, and inspiring to his men. He uses any and all resources at his disposal to ensure that he achieves his goals. Shakespeare presents Henry's charismatic ability to connect with his subjects and motivate them to embrace and achieve his goals as the fundamental criterion of good leadership, making Henry seem the epitome of a good leader. By inspiring his men to win the Battle of Agincourt despite overwhelming odds, Henry achieves heroic status.

But in becoming a great king, Henry is forced to act in a way that, were he a common man, might seem immoral and even unforgivable. In order to strengthen the stability of his throne, Henry betrays friends such as Falstaff, and he puts other friends to death in order to uphold the law. While it is difficult to fault Henry for having Scrope killed, since Scrope was plotting to assassinate him, Henry's cruel punishment of Bardolph is less understandable, as is his willingness to threaten the gruesome murder of the children of Harfleur in order to persuade the governor to surrender. Henry talks of favoring peace, but once his mind is settled on a course of action, he is willing to condone and even create massive and unprovoked violence in order to achieve his goal.

Shakespeare's portrayal of the king shows that power complicates the traditional distinctions between heroism and villainy, so that to call Henry one or the other constitutes an oversimplification of the issue. As Henry himself comments, the massive responsibilities laid on the shoulders of a king render him distinct from all other people, and the standards that can be brought to bear in judging a king must take that distinction into account. A king, in Shakespeare's portrayal, is responsible for the well-being and stability of his entire nation; he must subordinate his personal feelings, desires, dislikes, and even conscience wholly to this responsibility. Perhaps, then, the very nature of power is morally ambiguous, which would account for the implicit critique of Henry's actions that many contemporary readers find in the play. But within the framework of judgment suggested by the play, there is no doubt that Henry is both a great king and a hero.

THE DIVERSITY OF THE ENGLISH

The play opens with the Chorus reminding the audience that the few actors who will appear onstage represent thousands of their countrymen, and, indeed, the characters who appear in *Henry V* encompass the range of social classes and nationalities united under the English crown during Henry's reign. The play explores this breadth of humanity and the fluid, functional way in which the characters react to cultural differences, which melt or rupture depending on the situation.

The catalog of characters from different countries both emphasizes the diversity of medieval England and intensifies the audience's sense of Henry's tremendous responsibility to his nation. For a play that explores the nature of absolute political power, there is something remarkably democratic in this enlivening portrayal of rich and poor, English and Welsh, Scottish and Irish, as their roles intertwine in the war effort and as the king attempts to give them direction and momentum.

Interestingly, this disparate group of character types is not unanimous in supporting Henry. Many of them do admire the king, but other intelligent and courageous men, such as Michael Williams, distrust his motives. It is often seen as a measure of Henry's integrity that he is able to tolerate Williams's type of dissent with magnanimity, but the range of characters in the play would seem to imply that his tolerance is also expedient. With so many groups of individuals to take into account, it would be unrealistic of Henry to expect universal support—another measure of pressure added to his shoulders. In this way, the play's exploration of the people of Britain becomes an important facet of the play's larger exploration of power. As the play explores the ruler, it also examines the ruled.

THEMES

MOTIFS

Motifs are recurring structures, contrasts, or literary devices that can help to develop and inform the text's major themes.

MALE INTERACTION

There are almost no women in *Henry V*. Catherine is the only female character to be given many lines or presented in the domestic sphere, and most of her lines are in French. With this absence of women and the play's focus on the all-male activity of medieval warfare, the play presents many types of male relationships. The relationships between various groups of men—Fluellen and Gower; Bardolph, Pistol, and Nim; and the French lords—mirror and echo one another in various ways. The cowardice of the Eastcheap group is echoed in the cowardice of the French lords, for instance. Perhaps more important, these male friendships all draw attention to another aspect of Henry's character: his isolation from other people. Unlike most of the play's other male characters, Henry seems to have no close friends, another characteristic that makes the life of a king fundamentally different from the life of a common citizen.

PARALLELS BETWEEN RULERS AND COMMONERS

Henry V presents a wide range of common citizens. Some scenes portray the king's interactions with his subjects—Act IV, scene i, when Henry moves among his soldiers in disguise, is the most notable of these. The play also presents a number of mirror scenes, in which the actions of commoners either parallel or parody the actions of Henry and the nobles. Examples of mirror scenes include the commoners' participation at Harfleur in Act III, scene ii, which echoes Henry's battle speech in Act III, scene i, as well as Act II, scene i, where the commoners plan their futures, mirroring the graver councils of the French and English nobles.

WAR IMAGERY

The play uses a number of recurring metaphors for the violence of war, including images of eating and devouring, images of fire and combustion, and, oddly, the image of a tennis match. All of this imagery is rooted in aggression: in his rousing speech before the Battle of Harfleur, for example, Henry urges his men to become savage and predatory like tigers. Even the tennis balls, the silly gift from the Dauphin to Henry, play into Henry's aggressive war rhetoric. He states that the Dauphin's mocking renders the tennis balls "gun-stones," or cannonballs, thus transforming them from frivolous objects of play into deadly weapons of war (I.ii.282).

SYMBOLS

Symbols are objects, characters, figures, or colors used to represent abstract ideas or concepts.

THE TUN OF TENNIS BALLS

The Dauphin knows that Henry was an idler before becoming king, and he sends Henry a tun, or chest, of tennis balls to remind Henry of his reputation for being a careless pleasure-seeker. This gift symbolizes the Dauphin's scorn for Henry. The tennis balls enrage Henry, however, and he uses the Dauphin's scorn to motivate himself. The tennis balls thus come to symbolize Henry's burning desire to conquer France. As he tells the French ambassador, the Dauphin's jests have initiated a deadly match, and these tennis balls are now cannonballs.

CHARACTERS AS CULTURAL TYPES

As the Chorus tells the audience, it is impossible for a stage to hold the vast numbers of soldiers that actually participated in Henry V's war with France. As a result, many of the characters represent large groups or cultures: Fluellen represents the Welsh, Pistol represents the underclass, Jamy represents the Scottish, and MacMorris represents the Irish. These characters are often given the stereotypical traits thought to characterize each group in Shakespeare's day—MacMorris, for instance, has a fiery temper, a trait thought to be common to the Irish.

SYMBOLS

Summary & Analysis

Prologue and Act I, scene i

Summary: Prologue
The Chorus—a single character, whose speeches open each of the play's five acts—steps forward and announces that we are about to watch a story that will include huge fields, grand battles, and fighting kings. The Chorus notes, however, that we will have to use our imaginations to make the story come to life: we must imagine that the small wooden stage is actually the fields of France and that the few actors who will appear on the stage are actually the huge armies that fight to the death in those fields.

Summary: Act I, scene i
The Archbishop of Canterbury and the Bishop of Ely, two powerful English churchmen, confer with one another. They both express concern about a bill that has been brought up for the consideration of the king of England, Henry V. Canterbury and Ely don't want the king to pass this bill into law because it would authorize the government to take away a great deal of the church's land and money. The money would be used to maintain the army, support the poor, and supplement the king's treasury. The clergymen, who have been made wealthy and powerful by this land and money, naturally want to keep it for themselves.

In order to achieve his goal, the Archbishop of Canterbury has come up with a clever political strategy. The young King Henry V has been thinking about invading France, for he believes he has a claim to the throne of France as well. Canterbury anticipates that a war would distract the king from considering the bill to confiscate church property. So, to encourage Henry to concentrate on the invasion, Canterbury has made a promise to the king: he will raise a very large donation from the clergymen of the church to help fund the king's war efforts.

Canterbury and Ely also spend some time admiring the king's virtue and intelligence. They note that "[t]he courses of his youth promised it not" (I.i.25)—in other words, no one knew that the king would turn out so well, considering he wasted his adolescence taking part in "riots, banquets, [and] sports" (I.i.57) and hanging around with lowlifes. His reformation has been nothing short of miraculous. The new, improved Henry is about to meet with the delegation of French ambassadors who have come to England. Ely and Canterbury head for the throne room to participate in the meeting.

ANALYSIS: PROLOGUE AND ACT I, SCENE I

The Chorus, or Prologue, appears at the beginning of every act to introduce the action that follows, serving as a commentator as the action of the play progresses. Shakespeare frequently makes use of epilogues (as in *A Midsummer Night's Dream* and *The Tempest*), but the recurring Chorus is atypical for him. The Chorus serves a different purpose in every act, but its general role is to fire the audience's imagination with strong descriptive language that helps to overcome the visual limitations of the stage. At the start of Act I, the Chorus's specific purpose is to apologize for the limitations of the play that is to follow. This use of apology, usually as a means of encouraging the audience to express its approval, was a common technique in the drama of Shakespeare's time, though it was more often put into an epilogue that followed the play.

The Chorus's comments emphasize the fact that the play is a performance that requires the audience's mental cooperation to succeed. From the outset, the play suggests the impossibility of presenting the events as they really were, as the Chorus vainly wishes for "[a] kingdom for a stage, princes to act, / And monarchs to behold the swelling scene" (I.Prologue.3–4). But even as he (on Shakespeare's stage, a single actor would have played the Chorus) apologizes for the fact that his stage cannot show the full reality of events, the Chorus uses striking language to help the audience picture that reality for themselves: "Think, when we talk of horses, that you see them, / Printing their proud hoofs i'th' receiving earth" (I.Prologue.26–27). The Chorus's opening invocation of the muse, a classical figure of creative inspiration, also brings to mind the first lines of ancient epics of war, such as Virgil's *Aeneid*, and helps to situate *Henry V* within the imaginative tradition of ancient war epics that depict the deeds of great heroes. Shakespeare uses his most characteristic meter for the Chorus's speech: slightly irregular iambic pentameter—that is, lines composed of five feet, or groups of syllables, with the emphasis on the second syllable of each foot. The irregularities of the meter tend to call attention to certain important words and inject energy into the passage. The iambic pentameter continues as the action begins, although with far less rigor.

The conversation between Ely and Canterbury in Act I, scene i introduces the behind-the-scenes political intrigue that underlies the whole play and refers back to important events that have taken place before the play begins. Shakespeare's audiences would have been familiar with these historical events; in Shakespeare's time, as in Henry V's time (about 200 years earlier), the church was an extremely powerful and wealthy institution, second only to the monarchy in riches and influence. (In the play, however, the church in question is the Catholic Church, not the Church of England.) The church received much of its money from wealthy landowners who donated money just before they died, in the hopes that the church would pray for them and keep their souls from going to hell. Unfortunately, many leaders of the church were corrupt and worldly and spent church money on luxuries for themselves. Canterbury and Ely's greed and corruption in attempting to prevent passage of the bill—to avoid forfeiting lots of money by giving some money directly to the king—would have been obvious and familiar to Shakespeare's audience. Modern audiences may recognize the clergymen's tactics as an early example of a special interest group lobbying the government.

In the two *Henry IV* plays, the prequels to *Henry V*, Henry V appears as a wayward prince. The issue of his wayward youth and his reformation, introduced here by the clergymen, gets significant mention throughout *Henry V*. In fact, Henry's newly forged moral character, along with his suitability for the role of king, is perhaps the play's major focus. If Henry appears to be a drunken scoundrel in the *Henry IV* plays, he has now matured into an ideal English ruler who, good or bad, is a compelling figure. Unlike some of Shakespeare's other history plays, which focus on groups of historical figures, *Henry V* is very much a play about a single man.

Act I, scene ii

Summary: Act I, scene ii

And tell the pleasant Prince this mock of his
Hath turned his balls to gunstones, and his soul
Shall stand sore chargèd for the wasteful vengeance
That shall fly from them....

(See QUOTATIONS, *p. 48)*

In the throne room of the royal palace in England, King Henry V prepares to speak with a delegation of ambassadors from France. Several of his advisors and two of his younger brothers (Humphrey, duke of Gloucester, and Thomas, duke of Clarence) accompany him. Before speaking to the ambassadors, King Henry wants to talk to the representatives of the English Church, so he sends for the Archbishop of Canterbury and the Bishop of Ely.

King Henry asks Canterbury to explain to him, in clear and educated terms, the reasoning by which he, as king of England, has a rightful claim to the throne of France. This logic is complicated, going back several generations, and Henry wants to be able to justify a potentially bloody invasion. He reminds Canterbury of the responsibility that Canterbury himself will bear for the death toll of the war if he tells anything less than the truth, and he orders Canterbury to give him an honest opinion and faithful advice.

Canterbury gives the noblemen in the throne room a lengthy explanation of why Henry has a valid claim to France. In France, Canterbury explains, the throne cannot be inherited through a mother. That is, if a king has a daughter, the daughter's son has no claim to the throne. But England has no such law (known as Salic law in France), and kings can inherit the throne through the female line. Because King Henry's great-great-grandmother was a daughter of the king of France, under English law, he would be the rightful heir to the throne of France. Of course, the French don't think the same way, and they believe that their king, Charles VI, is the rightful monarch. If Henry wants to claim France, or even part of it, Canterbury concludes, he will have to invade and fight the French for it.

Both clergymen urge Henry to invade, as do his advisors, Exeter and Westmorland. Canterbury promises to raise from the clergymen a large war chest to finance the project (part of the self-interested plan he discusses in Act I, scene i). Henry expresses concern that the Scottish rebels on his northern border will invade while he is away, so Canterbury suggests that Henry take only one-quarter of his army with him to France, leaving the rest behind to defend England. Henry resolves to proceed with the invasion.

Finally, King Henry calls in the French ambassadors. They represent the Dauphin, the son of the king of France and, in the eyes of the French, the heir to the throne. The Dauphin's message is insulting: he laughs at Henry's claim to any part of France and says that Henry is still too young to be responsible. To top it off, he has sent the contemptuous gift of a container of tennis balls, mocking Henry's sportive and idle youth. Enraged, Henry gives the ambassadors a dark reply, warning them that the Dauphin has made a serious error in judgment, for Henry is not the foolish boy the Dauphin thinks he is. Henry declares his intent to invade and conquer France. The Dauphin will regret his mockery of the English king, he says, "[w]hen thousands weep more than did laugh at it" (I.ii.296).

ANALYSIS: ACT I, SCENE II

In his first scene, King Henry shows himself to be an intelligent, thoughtful, and efficient statesman, with an extremely impressive presence and a commitment to act as he believes right. He thinks carefully about whether or not to invade France, and although his decision seems to suit the clergymen very well, it is not clear that he has allowed them to manipulate him. More likely, his purposes simply coincide with theirs. Henry also shows his prudence when he absolves himself of potential blame by warning Canterbury very sternly that the lives lost in war must be on the archbishop's conscience if he misleads the king. The clean and regular meter of Henry's speech manifests his calm command of his subjects and his wits.

Canterbury's explanation of Salic law, though it is as clear as he can make it, nonetheless remains extremely complicated. Clearly, each side is interpreting ancient and confusing rules to its own advantage. Basically, the issue is whether the throne can or cannot be inherited through a female, but there is another issue as well. The old books that contain Salic law say that women cannot inherit in any "Salic land." The French interpret "Salic land" to mean France, but Canterbury thinks he has good evidence that this term actually refers to Germany, not France. Such an interpretation renders Henry's claim to the French throne valid.

The Dauphin's gag gift of tennis balls hinges on the ancient custom of sending a gift of treasure to a foreign ruler as a gesture of respect and friendship. On behalf of the Dauphin, the ambassador claims to present King Henry with a chest of treasure in exchange for Henry's abandonment of his claim to parts of France (apparently, Henry's early claims in France were limited to a few smaller regions, instead of the whole country). But the Dauphin, who has heard stories about King Henry's irresponsible teenage years, has sent tennis balls instead of anything valuable. The sarcastic spirit of this gift implies that the Dauphin considers the English king to be unworthy of an adult exchange.

In his reply to the ambassador, Henry turns the Dauphin's joke upside down. First he gives his thanks, starting his speech in a deceptively mild manner with the comment that "[w]e are glad the Dauphin is so pleasant with us" (I.ii.259). He then shows that he understands the Dauphin's insult, commenting, "[W]e understand [the Dauphin] well, / How he comes o'er us with our wilder days"— that is, how the Dauphin is trying to embarrass Henry with references to his wild youth (I.ii.266–267). Henry goes on to transform the game of tennis into a metaphor for a very real war, threatening, "When we have matched our rackets to these balls, / We will in France, by God's grace, play a set / Shall strike his father's crown into the hazard" (I.ii.261–263). He declares, in other words, that the war will be like a game, the spoils of which will be the kingship of France.

Moreover, Henry charges the Dauphin with responsibility for the impending devastation of France. Henry implies that this devastation will serve as revenge for the Dauphin's joke when he claims that

> This mock of his
> Hath turned his balls to gunstones, and his soul
> Shall stand sore chargèd for the wasteful vengeance
> That shall fly from them
>   (I.ii.281–284)

He claims that the Dauphin's mockery has provoked him to invade France, when, in fact, he has already decided on war before even admitting the French ambassadors. For the second time in this scene, Henry transfers responsibility for the deaths in the imminent war to someone else: first, he ascribes it to Canterbury, and now he ascribes it to the Dauphin. This strange evasion of responsibility, combined with Henry's willingness to accept Canterbury's corrupt and self-interested maneuvering, are among the many subtle criticism that Shakespeare injects into his portrayal of Henry as a heroic king. As the war proceeds, Henry assumes the dimensions of an epic hero, but Shakespeare occasionally implies that, beneath Henry's heroic status, his ethical status is somewhat dubious.

ACT II, PROLOGUE AND SCENES I–II

SUMMARY: ACT II, PROLOGUE

The Chorus introduces the second act, telling us that all of England is fired up and arming for the war, and King Henry is almost ready to invade France. But French agents have found some corrupt noblemen within the English ranks, and they have bribed them into acting as secret agents. These noblemen are Richard, earl of Cambridge; Henry Lord Scrope of Masham; and Sir Thomas Grey of Northumberland. This trio has agreed to kill King Henry in Southampton, just before he sets sail for France.

SUMMARY: ACT II, SCENE I

The scene shifts to London, near a tavern in Eastcheap, a seedy part of town. Lieutenant Bardolph and Corporal Nim appear, preparing to head off for the war. Both of these men are commoners, and Bardolph was once a criminal. Nim has a quarrel with a fellow soldier, Ancient Pistol. Pistol has married Mistress Quickly, the hostess of the Boar's Head Tavern in London, who had previously promised to marry Nim. Pistol and Nim draw their swords to attack each other and must be quieted several times by the hostess and Bardolph.

A boy, the page of a knight named Sir John Falstaff, appears. Falstaff, a close friend of everyone present, is old and very sick in bed, and the boy reports that he is getting worse. The hostess goes to see Falstaff and comes back to tell the others that he is dying. The men put aside their quarrel to go to visit him. Nim and Pistol speak darkly of something that King Henry has done to Falstaff; apparently, it is in some way the king's fault that Falstaff is on his deathbed.

SUMMARY: ACT II, SCENE II

In the port of Southampton, King Henry prepares his armies to sail for France. The conversation between Gloucester, Exeter, and Westmorland reveals that Henry has discovered the treachery of Cambridge, Scrope, and Grey, but the traitors don't know it yet. Henry enters with these same traitors, asking their advice on a case: a drunken man was arrested the previous day for speaking against

Henry in public. Henry plans to free him, but Cambridge, Scrope, and Grey advise him to punish the man instead.

King Henry decides to free the man anyway, and he lets Cambridge, Scrope, and Grey know that he has discovered their intended betrayal, handing them the incriminating evidence on paper. The three beg for mercy, but Henry is inflexible: he asks how they can possibly seek mercy for themselves when they think an ordinary drunkard deserves no mercy. Henry can barely believe that they would sell his life for money—especially Scrope, who has been a close friend—and orders the trio to be executed. Taking the discovery of the traitors as a sign that God is on the side of the English, Henry orders his fleet to sail for France at last.

ANALYSIS: ACT II, PROLOGUE AND SCENES I–II

The Chorus's introductory speech, which broadens the audience's perspective by presenting a big-picture view of the entire country in preparation for war, employs urgent and active language to heighten the sense that great deeds are afoot. A picture emerges of a country of heroes, ablaze with anticipation and activity: "Now all the youth of England are on fire, / ... / They sell the pasture now to buy the horse" (II.Prologue.1–5). Yet the individual soldiers-to-be that we encounter in Act II, scene i are much less awe-inspiring than those the Chorus describes. They speak in prose rather than verse, and they seem anything but heroic. The rhyming couplets with which Shakespeare ends important speeches are also absent in the speech of these commoners. However, the conflicts of the commoners often mirror those of the royals: Nim and Pistol argue over the rights to Mistress Quickly just as the kings argue over the rights to France.

Bardolph, Pistol, and the others (all the commoners but Nim) are veteran Shakespeare characters, introduced and developed in the Henry IV plays. In those plays, they take a secondary role to Sir John Falstaff, a larger-than-life comic creation and the bosom friend of the present-day King Henry, who is known in the Henry IV plays as Prince Hal. Falstaff does not appear onstage in *Henry V*, but the characters talk about him, and in Act II, scene iii we learn of his death.

Henry's history with Falstaff has important implications for Henry's character. Falstaff was a mentor and constant companion to Prince Hal before the death of his royal father, Henry IV. Much to Henry IV's chagrin, Falstaff taught the young Hal all about the underworld's way of life. When Prince Hal became king, though, he rejected Falstaff publicly. According to the friends who go to Falstaff's deathbed, this rejection was the beginning of the end for Falstaff. As the hostess explains it, Falstaff will die because "[t]he King has killed his heart" (II.i.79).

The juxtaposition of the announcement in Act II, scene i of Falstaff's impending death and the announcement in Act II, scene ii of Scrope's impending death creates an interesting implication—that the amount of power a person has plays an important role in determining what it is right or wrong for him to do. Falstaff, one of the king's former friends, is dying because Henry betrayed him. Scrope, another former friend, is also going to die, but because he betrayed Henry. There is a certain disturbing irony to this fact, but, at the same time, one of the reasons that power plays such a large role in determining a person's behavior is that with increased power comes an enlarged set of responsibilities. However he might have felt about Falstaff personally, Henry knew that Falstaff was a confirmed outlaw and thief and understood that keeping such a person close to the throne would not serve the larger needs of England. Along the same lines, it is likely that Henry conducts the execution of the traitorous noblemen as he does because he gives priority to his country's stability over the stability of his personal relationships. He considers it of utmost importance to send a signal to the other nobles that the war is a deadly serious business and will be conducted as such. Henry shows kindness when he can, freeing the insignificant drunkard, but when the fates of nations are at stake, he knows that he must act from motives larger than his own personal feelings. To spare Scrope out of love would weaken the stability of the throne. This sense of responsibility and the necessity of acting justly underlies Henry's apparent coldness. Henry himself later expounds upon this idea when he describes the pressures of living as a king.

Act II, scenes iii–iv

Summary: Act II, scene iii

Back in London, Pistol, Bardolph, Nim, and the hostess grieve over the death of Sir John Falstaff. The hostess describes his final moments. It seems that Falstaff was happy but also delirious at the very end. He said bad things about wine; no one can agree on whether or not he also cried out against women. Despite their sadness, the men must finally go off to the war, so Pistol kisses his wife, the hostess, and gives her advice and instructions for the time that he is away. He then heads off with the others, including Falstaff's newly masterless boy.

SUMMARY: ACT II, SCENE IV

Meanwhile, in France, Charles VI, the king of France, and his nobles and advisors discuss the approach of King Henry V's English forces. King Charles's eldest son, the Dauphin, still believes that Henry is the foolish and idle boy he once was. The Dauphin is eager to fight, but Charles, as well as the Constable of France, do not share his enthusiasm. They have spoken with the ambassadors who recently returned from England and are convinced of Henry's might. Charles also reminds the Dauphin that Henry's forebears have been fierce and victorious fighters against the French—especially Henry's great-grandfather, Edward III of England, and his son, Edward, Black Prince of Wales, who conquered the French at the Battle of Crécy (or Cressy).

The English nobleman Exeter arrives bearing a message from King Henry. Henry has already landed in France, and he now formally demands that King Charles yield up the crown of France and all the honors and land that go with it. If Charles refuses, Henry promises to invade France and take it by force. Exeter tells Charles to consider carefully and return an answer quickly. Charles says that in the morning he will send Exeter back to his king with an answer.

ANALYSIS: ACT II, SCENES III–IV

The famous description of Falstaff's death that the hostess gives in Act II, scene iii is odd and idiosyncratic, yet inadvertently very poignant. Her innocent foolishness infuses the passage with a sense of humor befitting Falstaff. When she says that Falstaff has gone "to Arthur's bosom" (II.iii.10), she is almost certainly making an error for the proverbial "Abraham's bosom." Yet it seems far more natural that Falstaff would join King Arthur after death than join Abraham, one of God's chosen. Perhaps the "green fields" that Falstaff babbles about as his death approaches are the fabled fields of a mythical and idealized England (II.iii.16–17). The hostess's accidental flippancy with regard to God is also unconsciously Falstaffian. The hostess says that when the dying Falstaff cried out "God, God, God," she "bid him … not think of God; I hoped there was no need to trouble himself with any such thoughts yet"

(II.iii.17–20). The gravity of the situation—Falstaff is dying, after all—is undermined by the foolishness of those in the scene.

Act II, scene iv is the first time in the play that we get the French point of view. As the climactic battle draws nearer, the play's point of view begins to alternate between the English and the French sides. We see that King Charles is prudent and wise in his estimation of King Henry. But to the Dauphin—Charles's son, and the heir to the French throne—Henry is still the "vain, giddy, shallow, humorous youth" that he has heard spoken of in the past (II.iv.28). Ironically, the Dauphin's attitude reveals only his own naïveté and youthfulness. The constable tries to point out the Dauphin's mistake, using a metaphor similar to that which the English clergymen employ in Act I, scene i: he states that Henry's wild early days were simply fertile soil for the mature flower of his kingship. He says that Henry's previous antics concealed his royal potential "[a]s gardeners do with ordure [manure] hide those roots / That shall first spring and be most delicate" (II.iv.39–40). While elder statesmen such as the constable and King Charles recognize Henry's true character, the stubborn Dauphin has to learn about it the hard way—through experience.

The message from King Henry that Exeter delivers to King Charles highlights Henry's skill with rhetoric. Henry's request for Charles to "[d]eliver up the crown, and to take mercy / On the poor souls for whom this hungry war / Opens his vasty jaws" simultaneously empowers and disempowers Charles (II.iv.103–105). These lines use a metaphor of devouring, one of the play's most common metaphors for war, to illustrate how helpless Charles and his countrymen will be in the face of the English army. Henry describes the war as "hungry" and having "vasty jaws" to make the war seem like a wild and unstoppable beast that will inevitably swallow France. At the same time, however, Henry offers Charles a way to avoid this catastrophe. His suggestion that Charles "take mercy" on his countrymen is cleverly worded, as the act of taking mercy on others requires being in power over others. Henry thus couches the unappetizing prospect of surrender in an appeal to Charles's kingly need to control. Once again, Henry's cleverness with words shows itself to be a powerful tool, although it is debatable whether Henry is an admirable strategist or a deceitful manipulator.

Act III, Prologue and scenes i–ii

Summary: Act III, Prologue

The Chorus describes the magnificence with which King Henry sails from England to France. We learn that Henry lands with a large fleet of warships at Harfleur, a port city on the northern coast of France. There, the English army attacks the city with terrifying force. The alarmed King Charles offers King Henry a compromise: he will not give him the crown of France, but he will give him some small dukedoms—that is, small sub-regions within France—as well as the hand of his daughter, Catherine, in marriage. But Henry rejects the offer, and the siege continues.

Summary: Act III, scene i

> Now set the teeth and stretch the nostril wide,
> Hold hard the breath, and bend up every spirit
> To his full height. On, on, you noblest English,
> Whose blood is fet from fathers of war-proof....
> *(See* QUOTATIONS, P. 49)

In the midst of the siege, King Henry appears to rally his soldiers. He delivers a powerful speech, conjuring up the memory of the Englishmen's warlike ancestors and appealing to soldiers, noblemen, and commoners alike.

Summary: Act III, scene ii

The scene shifts to Nim, Bardolph, Pistol, and the boy. Their conversation reveals that reception of the king's speech is rather mixed. Bardolph appears eager for the fight, but Nim, Pistol, and the boy are less happy about the idea of facing death. They wish they were safe back in London, drinking ale.

A superior officer notices the men loitering, and he beats them with a sword until they rush back into the fight. The officer, also in the service of King Henry, is a Welsh captain named Fluellen. The grown men run off, but the boy remains behind for a few moments to muse on the folly and hypocrisy of Nim, Bardolph, and Pistol. He declares that they are all cowards; he has learned this much in the time he has been serving them. He says that they want him to start learning to pick pockets and become a thief like them, but that such an idea is an affront to his manhood. He decides he must leave them and start looking for a better job.

ANALYSIS: ACT III, PROLOGUE AND SCENES I–II

King Henry's famous speech before the walls of Harfleur, which takes up all of Act III, scene i, is one of the most celebrated passages in the entire play. From his opening plea of "Once more unto the breach, dear friends, once more," Henry unifies his men for his cause (III.i.1). The whole of the stirring passage uses the techniques of poetry to celebrate and glorify war. In particular, Henry invokes images and metaphors from nature—of wild animals like the tiger and of natural forces like the weather—to urge his men to shift into a state of nearly uncontrolled ferocity for battle. His command to his men to "imitate the action of the tiger. / Stiffen the sinews, conjure up the blood, / Disguise fair nature with hard-favoured rage" is a call to arms, a call for his men to display their masculinity (III.i.5–8).

In his speech, Henry also uses two other inspirational tactics. First, he invokes English patriotism, calling upon "you, good yeomen, / Whose limbs were made in England," to "show us here / The mettle of your pasture; let us swear / That you are worth your breeding" (III.i.25–28). Henry's exploitation of patriotism is a two-part process: he exalts all things English and then compels his soldiers to prove that they are worthy Englishmen. In so doing, and in reminding his men of their warlike ancestors and great historical battles, he attempts to rouse nationalist fervor among his men and a sense of pride in them about their glorious heritage. Second, Henry takes a nontraditional democratic stance, expressing an egalitarian view of soldiering by saying that every soldier is as good as a nobleman: "For there is none of you so mean and base / That hath not noble lustre in your eyes" (III.i.29–30). With these words, Henry endows his men with an elevated stature, which he hopes will compel them to act in an elevated manner.

Henry V seems to celebrate and glorify war, a fact that bothers some critics and readers. However, Henry is careful to note that people should not be fighters all the time; he often states that peace is better than war. His message, then, is that when men have to fight, they should do it with full force. In the Harfleur speech, for instance, he begins by saying that "[i]n peace there's nothing so becomes a man / As modest stillness and humility," before he goes on to talk of war (III.i.3–4). Earlier passages, such as Henry's speech to Canterbury in Act I, scene ii, or the message he sends with Exeter in Act II, scene iv, illustrate that Henry likes to present himself as a basically peaceful king who has been forced into making war. This stance can be viewed as hypocrisy, however, since Henry is the one invading France. Similarly, Henry's actions in the play do not reflect the "modest stillness and humility" he claims to prize (III.i.4). Still, one can argue that *Henry V* does not celebrate war so much as it celebrates Henry and his skillful political ability, which happens to involve using war to achieve his desired ends.

ACT III, SCENES III–V

SUMMARY: ACT III, SCENE III

Captain Fluellen enters with Captain Gower, his fellow officer and friend. Gower and Fluellen discuss the "mines," or tunnels, that the English side has dug in order to get under the walls of Harfleur (III.iii.4). Fluellen, who is well informed about the ancient Roman tactics of war, thinks that the mines are being dug incorrectly. In his characteristically amusing and very wordy manner, Fluellen expresses his scorn for Captain MacMorris, the Irish officer in charge of digging the mines, and his admiration for Captain Jamy, the officer in charge of the Scottish troops.

Captain MacMorris and Captain Jamy enter, and Fluellen offers MacMorris some advice about digging the tunnels. The hotheaded MacMorris takes offense, and they begin to quarrel. But they are all responsible officers, and there is much work to be done, so after some philosophizing about the hazards of war and the inevitability of death, all four head back into the battle.

With a flourish of trumpets, King Henry appears before the gates of the French town of Harfleur. The town has sounded a parley—in other words, its inhabitants have asked for a cease-fire in order to negotiate. The governor of Harfleur stands on the town walls. King Henry addresses him, advising him to surrender immediately. Henry declares that if the governor surrenders, the people of the town will be allowed to live; if he makes the English fight their way inside, however, the English will destroy the town, rape the women, and kill the children. The governor replies that although he would rather not surrender, he has just received word from the Dauphin that no army can be raised in time to rescue Harfleur. He declares that he will therefore open the gates. Henry orders Exeter to fortify Harfleur as a citadel from which the English can fight the French. He says that he himself will take his forces onward to Calais the next day.

SUMMARY: ACT III, SCENE IV

In King Charles's palace, Charles's daughter, Catherine, speaks with her maid, Alice. Catherine speaks no English, and this scene is spoken almost entirely in French. Alice has spent some time in England and knows some English, and so Catherine asks Alice to teach her the language. Catherine seems to suspect, wisely, that she may soon need to be able to communicate with the king of England. They begin by learning the names of parts of the body. Catherine mispronounces them amusingly, but she is eager to learn them anyway—that is, until the final two words, "foot" and "cown" (gown), which sound like French obscenities.

SUMMARY: ACT III, SCENE V

Elsewhere at the French court, King Charles, the Dauphin, and his advisors—including the Constable of France and the Duke of Bourbon—are having an urgent meeting to discuss King Henry's swift advance through France. The French exclamations that pepper their English conversation signify the degree of their distress. They cannot figure out how the English got to be so courageous, since they come from such a damp, gloomy climate. They feel their national honor has been outraged by the British successes, and they are determined to turn the tables. Worst of all, their wives and mistresses have started to make fun of them for being beaten by King Henry's forces.

King Charles, more sensible and decisive than his followers, orders all his noblemen to raise troops for the army. He calls on about twenty noblemen by name, and presumably there are many more. Charles and his men are confident that with this great number of troops raised, they can intimidate King Henry, conquer his army, and bring him back as a defeated prisoner.

ANALYSIS: ACT III, SCENES III–V

On the battlefield, a new set of important characters enters the play: the foreign soldiers fighting under King Henry's rule, men who come from the countries that border England and are under English control. Captain Fluellen is from Wales (his name is an Anglicized spelling of the still-common Welsh name Llewellyn), Captain Jamy is from Scotland, and Captain MacMorris is from Ireland. They all speak with distinctive accents, and their personality traits and linguistic idiosyncrasies reflect Renaissance English ideas about the national character of these other countries. Captain MacMorris is hot-tempered, for example, and Captain Fluellen is thoughtful and didactic. Shakespeare uses this extraordinary linguistic and cultural diversity to present a broad cross section of the British people in the throes of war.

King Henry urges the surrender of Harfleur with the same complex, morally shaky rhetoric that we see in earlier scenes. He plans— or at least claims to plan, in order to intimidate the governor—to authorize rape, murder, and total destruction unless the governor surrenders the city. The images Henry uses are vivid: he tells the governor to imagine "[t]he blind and bloody soldier with foul hand / Defil[ing] the locks of your still-shrieking daughters" (III.iii.111– 112) and "[y]our naked infants spitted upon pikes" (III.iii.115). These images, in addition to being highly disturbing, are troublesome in that they force us to question how honorable or decent Henry is if he is willing to harm innocents so cruelly. Furthermore, Henry's speech once again deflects responsibility for the impending carnage from himself. He says that if the town doesn't surrender instantly, he will lose control of his soldiers, and it will be Harfleur's own fault for subjecting itself to destruction and rape. This idea seems to be mere rhetoric, however, as it is Henry who has urged his men to become killing machines, and Henry who has the power to sway them from acting savagely.

Shortly after the introduction of the dialects of Fluellen, Mac-Morris, and Jamy, Shakespeare adds another level to his increasingly complicated linguistic panorama by rendering Act III, scene iv almost entirely in French. The scene is essentially a comic one, a language lesson mangled by the deficiency of the teacher, Alice. A further source of humor is Catherine's perception of apparent obscenities in basic English words. Catherine is scandalized by the similarity of "foot" to the French word "foutre," meaning "to fuck." Similarly, "cown," Alice's pronunciation of "gown," sounds to Catherine like the French word "con," or "cunt." Catherine declares that she is disgusted with English—a language that is vulgar and immodest ("gros, et impudique") and that respectable ladies would not use (III.iv.48).

In Act III, scene v, we see that the French nobility are at last starting to take the threat of Henry's invasion seriously. Still, instead of being threatened by the English troops' show of power, all of the Frenchmen except King Charles are simply scornful, scandalized that the English have been allowed to progress so far. Shakespeare throws in an assortment of French phrases to show the agitation of the group as well as to accent their foreignness. The noblemen exclaim, "O Dieu vivant!" ("O living God!"), "Mort de ma vie!" ("Death of my life!"), and "Dieu de batailles!" ("O God of battles!"—a phrase Henry himself uses later on). They deride and insult the English with amusing turns of phrase that make them seem more like mocking schoolboys than warriors. By portraying the Frenchmen's petty mockery of the English, Shakespeare ironically mocks the French.

ACT III, SCENES VI–VII

SUMMARY: ACT III, SCENE VI

After the English take Harfleur, the Welsh Captain Fluellen talks with the English Captain Gower about the battle for a bridge that is currently taking place. Ancient Pistol enters with a favor to beg of Fluellen. Pistol's good friend and fellow soldier Bardolph, has been found guilty of stealing from the conquered French town. He has stolen a "pax," a tablet made out of some valuable material and used in religious rites (III.vi.35).

Bardolph has been sentenced to death by hanging, since that is the punishment Henry has decreed for looters. Pistol begs Fluellen to intercede with the Duke of Exeter to save Bardolph's life, but Fluellen politely refuses, saying that discipline must be maintained. Despairing, Pistol curses Fluellen, makes an obscene gesture at him, and stalks away.

Gower, who has watched the whole exchange, realizes that he recognizes Pistol and tells Fluellen that he has met Pistol before. Pistol, Gower says, is the kind of man who only goes off to war now and then but pretends to be a full-time soldier when he is back home. Fluellen says that he will keep an eye on Pistol and try to detect his deceptions.

With a drumroll and fanfare, King Henry enters. He questions Fluellen about the battle for the bridge and about how many soldiers the English side lost in the last skirmish. Fluellen answers that, thanks to the smart fighting of the Duke of Exeter, the English have won the bridge. Amazingly, no English soldiers have been lost—except Bardolph, who has been sentenced to hang for stealing. At this news, King Henry displays no visible emotion (which is somewhat surprising, given that when Henry was a prince, he and Bardolph were friends). Henry merely voices his approval of the punishment, stressing how important it is that the conquered French, and their property, be treated with the utmost respect.

Montjoy, a French messenger, arrives with a deeply menacing message from the king of France. King Charles declares that the time has come for him to punish the overly proud King Henry. He suggests that Henry start thinking about his "ransom"—the recompense that the French will demand for their losses when they defeat the English king (III.vi.113).

King Henry sends back a surprisingly even-tempered reply. He admits that his army has tired and that he would rather not fight the French if he can avoid it. He states, however, that he will continue to march on because he believes he is in the right and that he thinks that he will eventually be victorious. Montjoy departs, and the English camp goes to sleep for the night.

SUMMARY: ACT III, SCENE VII

In the French camp, several French noblemen—including the Duke of Orléans, the Constable of France, and Lord Rambures—discuss the upcoming battle. The Duke of Orléans brags about his horse, and the others tease him. After a while, a messenger enters to say that the English army is camped nearby. The French nobles then start making fun of King Henry and the Englishmen.

ANALYSIS: ACT III, SCENES VI–VII

The events of Act III, scene vi may seem a trivial digression, but they actually contribute to one of the play's main concerns: the extent to which Henry has developed from a frivolous youth into a disciplined leader. The salient fact is that Henry actually knows the thieving soldier Bardolph very well. In the old days, when Henry was still Prince Hal, his closest companions were Falstaff and his crew—including Bardolph. King Henry fought, drank, and even robbed with Bardolph in 1 *Henry IV*. Knowing this history of camaraderie, we might expect Henry to pardon his old friend. Yet King Henry condemns Bardolph to death with apparent coldness. Gone is the self-professed sense of mercy with which Henry sets the treasonous drunkard free in Act II, scene ii. His decree here that "[w]e would have all such offenders so cut off"—meaning that all looters should be hanged—shows just how severe a man Henry has become (III.vi.98).

Though Henry's impersonal treatment of his former friend may appear unattractively ruthless, Shakespeare may also be making the point that good leadership entails putting personal feelings aside. In a monarchy, the king is the sole source of law and stability for his nation; Henry realizes that he has a higher duty to the law than he does to his personal friendship with Bardolph, just as he had a higher duty to the law than he did to Falstaff or Scrope. Henry may be waging a violent and bloody war to seize the throne of France, but he acts more as an unstoppable moral force than as the leader of a usurping army. Henry is willing to wage war because he believes himself to be the legitimate king of France; as the king of France, he will hang thieves, whether he knows them personally or not.

The frustration that Pistol directs at Fluellen might more properly be directed at Henry himself, but even if Pistol had the opportunity to complain to the king, he would pay for doing so. He certainly would never cry out "Die and be damned! and fico for thy friendship" to the king, as he does to Fluellen (III.vi.51). The gesture accompanying the word "fico," which means "fig" in Spanish, consists of thrusting the thumb between two other fingers. This gesture is obscene, with roughly the same meaning to Elizabethan audiences as "the finger" has to modern Americans.

Act III, scene vii, which presents the French side of the battlefield, injects some comic relief into a very tense buildup to battle. The scene also portrays the arrogance and frivolity of the French nobility, which contrasts sharply with King Henry's steady and deadly focus. Whereas on the English side we see commoners—Pistol and Nim, and even Fluellen and Gower—we see no such counterparts on the French side. Shakespeare thus adds to the impression that all the French are decadent noblemen, like the Duke of Orléans.

ACT IV, PROLOGUE AND SCENES I–II

SUMMARY: ACT IV, PROLOGUE

The Chorus describes the scene in the French and English camps the night before the battle: the quiet night, the burning watch fires, the clank of the knights being suited up in their armor. In the French camp, the overly confident officers have already decided how to divide up the loot of the English, for they outnumber the English by five to one. In the English camp, the soldiers all believe that they will die the next morning, but they wait patiently for their fate. During the night, King Henry goes out among his soldiers, visiting all of them, calling them brothers and cheering them up. This visit raises morale greatly, for every soldier is pleased to see, as the Chorus puts it, "[a] little touch of Harry in the night" (IV.Prologue.47).

SUMMARY: ACT IV, SCENE I

> *The slave, a member of the country's peace,*
> *Enjoys it, but in gross brain little wots*
> *What watch the King keeps to maintain the peace,*
> *Whose hours the peasant best advantages.*
>
> *(See* QUOTATIONS, *p. 50)*

At the English camp at Agincourt, King Henry talks briefly with his brothers, Gloucester and Clarence, and with old Sir Thomas Erpingham. He asks to borrow Erpingham's dirty cloak, then sends these advisors off to confer with the other noblemen in his royal tent, claiming that he wants to be alone for a while.

Wrapped anonymously in the borrowed cloak, Henry sits by the common campfire, talking with whoever wanders by. He is pretending to be an ordinary soldier, and none of the men recognizes him as the king. The first person to come by is Pistol. When Henry brings up the subject of the king, Pistol praises Henry, in his own rough and bizarre way. Pistol then insults Fluellen, and Henry, going under the name Harry le Roy (le roi, French for "the king"), humorously pretends to be Fluellen's relative. Pistol promptly gives him the obscene fico gesture and leaves.

Next to come by are Fluellen and Gower, but they are so busy talking to each other that neither of them sees Henry. Gower greets Fluellen, but Fluellen scolds him to talk more softly while they are so close to the enemy. Henry silently admires Fluellen's prudence and intelligence.

Next, three common soldiers—John Bates, Alexander Court, and Michael Williams—join Henry at the campfire. Henry discusses with them the English troops' odds in the coming battle and finds that they doubt the motives and the courage of the king (these men, of course, do not recognize Henry). Henry defends the absent king, but Williams will not back down, so they agree to establish a quarrel. They exchange gloves, signaling their intent to find each other later and fight if they both survive the battle.

The three soldiers leave, and Henry muses to himself. He laments the lonely isolation of power, which is combined with the need to be eternally vigilant. The only consolation Henry can see in being king is the elaborate ceremony and costuming that accompanies the position. Yet he contends that this ceremony is empty and that he would rather be a slave, who is at least able to rest easy and not worry about the safety of his country.

It is nearly dawn and almost time for the battle. Henry, still alone, prays to God to strengthen the hearts of his soldiers. He also entreats God not to punish him for the bloody manner by which his own father took the English crown, to Henry's shame and regret.

SUMMARY: ACT IV, SCENE II

Meanwhile, at their camp, the French prepare for the battle. The constable, Lord Rambures, the Earl of Grandpré, and others put on their armor and mount their horses. The constable and Grandpré give pre-battle speeches full of confidence and cheerfulness. Seeing the English army's ragged appearance and small numbers, the French look forward to an easy victory.

ANALYSIS: ACT IV, PROLOGUE AND SCENES I–II

Henry's disguised conversations with his soldiers in Act IV, scene i demonstrate the closeness between king and commoner. The scene quickly runs through the many different kinds of voices that sound in *Henry V*, showing how each of them interacts with Henry and thus adding a new dimension to our understanding of the formidable monarch. Henry's conversations with his soldiers highlight the commonalities between king and subject, as does the fact that, without the costume of kingship, Henry is not recognizable as a king. Henry speaks to his similarity to other men when he tells his soldiers that "I think the King is but a man, as I am. The violet smells to him as it doth to me. . . . His ceremonies laid by, in his nakedness he appears but a man" (IV.i.99–102). Henry clearly understands that the difference between him and other men lies only in the trappings of his position—he may be wealthy and powerful, but flowers smell the same to him as they do to everyone else.

At the same time, one can argue that because most of the soldiers don't even know what Henry looks like well enough to recognize him in the flesh, this scene underscores the distance between the king and his soldiers as much as it emphasizes the similarities between them. When Henry is alone again, his thoughts turn to the differences between his position and that of the common soldiers. In a monologue of central importance to his character, Henry describes the terrible responsibilities of power, which both isolate and weigh upon the king. Everybody seems to lay all their worries, concerns, and guilt upon the shoulders of the king, who has nothing to ease this terrible responsibility except an empty display of power and glory. "What infinite heartsease / Must kings neglect that private men enjoy?" Henry asks, offering us a rare perspective on the negative aspect of power and demonstrating his understanding of the distance between himself and his men (IV.i.218–219).

Henry's comment that "thrice-gorgeous ceremony / . . . / Can[not] sleep so soundly as the wretched slave" closely echoes a speech given by his own father in Shakespeare's 2 Henry IV (IV.i.248–250). That speech, which ends with the famous line "Uneasy lies the head that wears a crown," expresses the weary Henry IV's understanding of the responsibilities of power, which the young Henry V, like his father before him, must now learn (2 Henry IV, III.i.31). This speech by Henry V is crucially important to the play, as it finds Henry alone for the first time; it is our first opportunity to get a glimpse into Henry's psyche that is not compromised by his need to appear kingly. Henry presents us with the idea that his motivation for his actions as king is not power-lust or arrogance, but simply a crushing sense of responsibility to preserve stability and order for his subjects.

The conversation among Henry and John Bates, Alexander Court, and Michael Williams marks the first time we hear from English soldiers who do not completely support King Henry. Williams's argument that the soldiers do not know whether or not the king's reasons for being in France are particularly worthy is a powerful one, and it is likely to match our own reservations about Henry as a hero. Williams claims that:

> If the [King's] cause be not good, the King himself hath a heavy reckoning to make, when all those legs and arms and heads chopped off in a battle shall join together at the latter day [Judgment Day], and cry all, 'We died at such a place'— some swearing, some crying for a surgeon, some upon their wives left poor behind them . . . some upon their children rawly left. I am afeard there are few die well that die in a battle.
> (IV.i.128–135)

Throughout the play, Henry has been arguing that he is in no way to blame for damage caused by his war, but Williams challenges Henry's claims, arguing that the king has the greatest moral responsibility. In doing so, Williams evokes the image of the shattered family, just as Henry does in Act III, scene iii, when he threatens the town of Harfleur.

Yet, even in disguise, Henry continues to deny all responsibility on behalf of the king. In his answer, Henry ignores most of Williams's argument, choosing to focus his rebuttal on Williams's statement that men who die in battle die badly—that is, die in sin and are condemned to hell. This technical religious point is largely tangential to Williams's argument. Henry ignores the larger question of whether the king is responsible for his soldiers' deaths. Henry seems really to believe in Canterbury's legal justification for his invasion of France. Moreover, he seems really to believe himself the king of France and that the man currently sitting on the throne is not the real king. Because he writes off the invasion as justified and ordained by God, Henry doesn't concern himself—or, at least, he feels that he is not required to concern himself—with the issue of his moral responsibility.

Henry's belief in his right to the throne of France may seem dubious to modern readers—it makes little sense that a bloody war in which an invading foreign monarch conquers another culture could really reestablish the proper order of things. Indeed, even Shakespeare seems to question Henry's logic at times. But it is important to remember that although Shakespeare definitely allows for an ironic, or critical, reading of Henry's actions, Henry's thinking is not out of line with the ideas of the post-medieval era. Therefore, it is not fair to write off Henry's certainty that he is blameless as a mere disguise for insatiable power-lust.

Finally, Henry's heartfelt prayer at the end of the scene gives us an interesting glimpse into one of his insecurities. He nurses a lasting concern over the dubious way his own father, Henry IV, got the crown—a process that included the overthrow and murder of the previous king, Richard II. (Shakespeare covers these events in the first play of the tetralogy, Richard II.) Henry V has tried to atone for Richard's death with purchased prayers, but he still seems to be haunted by it, a doubt that makes sense given Henry's own intractable notions of the rights of kingship and his own unbending certainty that he is the true king of France. After all, under Henry's logic, if his father stole his crown, then he is not the true king even of England.

ACT IV, SCENES III–V

SUMMARY: ACT IV, SCENE III

> *If we are marked to die, we are enough*
> *To do our country loss; and if to live,*
> *The fewer men, the greater share of honour.*
> *(See* QUOTATIONS, *p. 52)*

The English noblemen, gathering before the Battle of Agincourt, realize that the French outnumber them five to one. Westmorland wishes that they had with them some of the men who sit idle in England. But King Henry, entering and overhearing him, disagrees. In his famous St. Crispin's Day speech (so called because he addresses his troops on October 25, St. Crispin's Day), King Henry says that they should be happy that there are so few of them present, for each can earn a greater share of honor.

Henry goes on to say that he does not want to fight alongside any man who does not wish to fight with the English. He tells the soldiers that anyone who wants to leave can and will be given some money to head for home. But anyone who stays to fight will have something to boast about for the rest of his life and in the future will remember with pride the battle on this day. He adds that every commoner who fights today with the king will become his brother, and all the Englishmen who have stayed at home will regret that they were not in France to gain honor upon this famous day of battle. The soldiers and noblemen are greatly inspired, and morale rises dramatically.

The French are now ready for the battle. Montjoy, the French messenger, comes to the English camp one more time, asking King Henry if he wants to take the last opportunity for peace and surrender himself for ransom, instead of facing certain defeat in battle. Henry rejects the offer in strong though courteous terms, and the English organize and march into battle.

SUMMARY: ACT IV, SCENE IV

As the battle rages across the field, Pistol takes a French prisoner. The scene is comic: Pistol, who cannot speak French, tries to communicate with the Frenchman, who cannot speak English. Fortunately, the boy is present. He speaks very good French and is able to translate, though the hotheaded Pistol makes communication difficult. The terrified soldier is convinced that Pistol is a nobleman and a ferocious fighter.

The French soldier, who gives his name as Monsieur le Fer, says that he is from a respected house and family and that his relatives will give Pistol a rich ransom if Pistol will let him live. Pistol is very interested in money and accepts this bargain, and the grateful Frenchman surrenders as a willing captive. As the boy follows them offstage, he complains about Pistol's empty boasting, saying that Bardolph and Nim both had ten times as much real courage in them as Pistol. The boy reveals a surprising and unsettling fact: Nim, like Bardolph, has been hanged for stealing.

SUMMARY: ACT IV, SCENE V

The French camp is in disarray, and the French soldiers' cries reveal that, against all expectations, the English have won the day. The French troops have been routed and scattered. Astonished and dismayed, the French nobles bewail their great shame and contemplate suicide. But they decide that rather than surrender in shame and defeat, they will go down fighting and return to the field for one final attempt.

ANALYSIS: ACT IV, SCENES III–V

King Henry's inspirational St. Crispin's Day speech—so called because the battle is fought on the feast day of St. Crispin, a holiday in the England of the play—is perhaps the most famous passage in the play. In this speech, which is meant to bolster the morale of his soldiers before they head into a battle that they are almost certain to lose, Henry demonstrates his customary brilliance with words and astounding charisma, both of which he has displayed so often before.

Henry's challenge is to turn his troops' small numbers into an advantage, which he does by convincing his men that the battle is more than a mathematical formula, that they have all come there to fight for honor, for justice, and for glory. He makes fighting with him at Agincourt sound like a privilege, one that will allow its participants to capture more glory than anything else could. Henry also brings up, once more, the motif of the bond between king and commoner. As in Act III, scene i, before the Battle of Harfleur, he unites himself with his men, saying,

> We few, we happy few, we band of brothers.
> For he today that sheds his blood with me
> Shall be my brother; be he ne'er so vile,
> This day shall gentle his condition....
>   (IV.III.60–63)

Henry claims that even a commoner will be made noble by fighting at his side and that the result will be lifelong honor that will elevate these fighters above their peers.

The comic scene of Pistol's capture of a Frenchman plays on language in much the same way that the earlier scene of Catherine's English lesson does. Pistol's misunderstandings of French, like Catherine's of English, are amusing. He takes the soldier's exclamation, "O Seigneur Dieu!" ("O Lord God!"), for a name and mistakes the words "bras" ("arm") and "moi" ("me") for "brass" and "moy" (a unit of measurement). Pistol must rely on the boy to translate for him, and, ironically, the boy shows himself to be better informed than the man he serves.

In the jaws of defeat, the French noblemen at long last recognize the power of the English combatants. When they realize that their troops have been scattered and defeated, their first reaction is one of overwhelming shame. But the nobles show a hitherto unprecedented courage when they decide to return to the fight instead of surrendering, as they might, and giving themselves up to be ransomed. This last show of courage on the part of the French adds a welcome new dimension to Shakespeare's characterization of different nationalities and prevents his portrayal of the French from becoming a one-dimensional mockery motivated only by patriotic loyalty to England.

ACT IV, SCENES VI–VIII

SUMMARY: ACT IV, SCENE VI

On the field at the Battle of Agincourt, the English appear to have seized the advantage and have captured many French soldiers and noblemen. But the battle is not quite over, as many of the French continue to fight. Exeter gives King Henry an update on the battle: the English are doing well, but two noble cousins, the Duke of York and the Earl of Suffolk, have been killed. Exeter touchingly describes the way the wounded York lay down to die beside the body of his beloved cousin Suffolk. Henry, like Exeter, is moved to tears by the story.

A sudden stir and cry sounds. King Henry, interpreting this commotion as a rally by the French, abruptly orders every English soldier to kill his French prisoners—a remarkably bloody move.

SUMMARY: ACT IV, SCENE VII

Alexander, God knows, and you know … did in his ales and his angers, look you, kill his best friend Cleitus—
(See QUOTATIONS, *p. 53)*

Back in the press of battle, Fluellen talks with Gower. A small group of French soldiers, fleeing the main crush of the battle, have attacked the English camp. They have looted the goods there and murdered the young pages, mere children, who were left in the camp. Fluellen is outraged at the French atrocity of killing the young pages, which violates the chivalrous codes of battle. He agrees with Gower in approving of King Henry's decision to slaughter the French prisoners, and he compares the valiant Henry to Alexander the Great.

King Henry appears, with the Duke of Bourbon as a prisoner. Having learned about the slaughter of the boys, he says he is angrier than he has ever been before and repeats the order to kill the French prisoners. Montjoy, the now-humbled French messenger, reappears. He brings a request from the king of France that the French be allowed to go safely into the battlefield to identify, recover, and bury their dead. King Henry demands to know whether the English won. Montjoy says they have, and Henry praises God for the victory.

Henry spots the soldier Michael Williams, with whom he argued and exchanged gloves the night before. Henry decides to play a practical joke: he gives Williams's glove to Fluellen and tells him to wear it publicly, saying that it came from a noble Frenchman in the field and that anyone who attacks Fluellen over it must be a traitor to the English. Henry then follows them to see the fun.

SUMMARY: ACT IV, SCENE VIII

When Williams sees Fluellen, he recognizes his own glove and thinks Fluellen was the man with whom he quarreled the night before. He strikes Fluellen, and Fluellen, believing that Williams is a French traitor, orders him to be arrested. King Henry arrives, innocently asking about the cause of the fuss, and then he reveals to Williams that his quarrel is really with King Henry himself. Williams says that he cannot be held responsible for picking a quarrel with the king because Henry was deliberately disguising his identity the preceding night. Henry, enjoying his little joke and approving of Williams's courage, rewards him by filling his glove with coins.

Exeter and a herald return to report the total number of casualties. Ten thousand French soldiers are dead, but somehow the English have lost only twenty-nine men. Recognizing their extraordinary good luck, the Englishmen give praise to God. Henry orders his men to proceed to the captured village, but without any bragging.

ANALYSIS: ACT IV, SCENES VI–VIII
The touching story of the death of the Duke of York, which Exeter relates to Henry at the beginning of Act IV, scene vi, presents a very romanticized view of death in battle. Both Exeter and Henry are deeply touched by the great love between York and his cousin Suffolk, as well as by York's selfless courage and love for his king. The discrepancy between York and Suffolk's devoted friendship and King Henry's ill fated friendships—with Falstaff, Scrope, and Bardolph, for instance—highlights again the pressure of monarchy, which prevents Henry from enjoying such an uncomplicated, loving friendship with anyone.

The problems inherent in loving Henry are raised again in the following scene, in the conversation between Fluellen and Gower. Fluellen's comparison of King Henry to Alexander the Great is evidently meant to be very flattering, but it does not exactly come off that way. Fluellen begins by referring to "Alexander the Pig" (IV.vii.12–13). Of course, he means to say "Alexander the Big"—an error for "Alexander the Great," as Gower promptly corrects him—but Fluellen's Welsh accent turns the b into a p.

Moreover, the qualities Fluellen praises in Alexander do not necessarily seem flattering when applied to Henry. The most telling of these comes when Fluellen mentions that Alexander, "in his rages and his furies ... did in his ales and his angers ... kill his best friend Cleitus" (IV.vii.28–32). The parallel Fluellen has in mind is that Henry, at the same age (twenty-eight) Alexander was when he killed Cleitus, "turned away the fat knight with the great-belly doublet" (IV.vii.40). Gower supplies the knight's name: Sir John Falstaff. This memory does not seem to diminish Henry in Fluellen's eyes, but it may not sit as comfortably with the audience. Shakespeare continually reminds us that the nature of kingship is such that being a good king may keep one from being a likable man.

The discrepancy revealed in the numbers of the French and the English dead (10,000 versus twenty-nine) may seem almost impossible to believe. Nonetheless, these seem to be the real numbers for the historical battle of Agincourt—at least, they are the numbers recorded for the Battle of Agincourt in Shakespeare's historical source, the Chronicles of Raphael Holinshed. One cause of the high French mortality rate is that the French army lost its organization, and many of the French soldiers broke and ran. In flight, they were easy targets and couldn't fight back very well. It had rained very heavily prior to the battle, putting the French, with their heavy armor and horses, at a disadvantage. But probably the most important cause of the lopsided victory was the English use of the longbow, a weapon that had existed for hundreds of years but whose use had been forgotten on the continent until the English brought it to Agincourt. Shakespeare, however, does not attribute the outcome of the battle to tactics, weather, or technology, preferring to depict Henry's victory as an act of God.

ACT V, PROLOGUE, SCENES I–II, AND EPILOGUE

SUMMARY: ACT V, PROLOGUE

The Chorus relates that King Henry has returned to the port city of Calais in France and, from there, has sailed back to England. The women and children of England are overjoyed to have their men returned to them, and everyone is also glad to see King Henry. When Henry returns to London, the people flock to see him and to celebrate. But Henry is humble and forbids a triumphal procession to celebrate his victory.

Henry returns to France again, and the Chorus orders the audience to return its imagination to France, with the understanding that some time has passed.

SUMMARY: ACT V, SCENE I

Fluellen and Gower converse at an English army base in France. Gower is curious about why Fluellen still wears a leek in his hat, since St. Davy's Day was the previous day. (St. Davy is the patron saint of Wales, and on St. Davy's Day, March 1, Welsh people traditionally wear a leek in their hats as a show of patriotism.)

Fluellen explains that, the day before, the obnoxious soldier Pistol insulted him by sending him bread and salt and suggesting that Fluellen eat his leek. So, when Pistol appears, Fluellen starts to beat him with his cudgel until Pistol agrees to the condition that will satisfy Fluellen's pride: Pistol himself must eat the leek that Fluellen has been carrying in his hat. Pistol eats the leek, and Fluellen gives him some money to ease the pain of his cudgel wounds. After Fluellen leaves, Pistol vows revenge for having been force-fed the leek, but Gower says it was Pistol's own fault for making fun of Fluellen—and for underestimating him simply because he speaks with a funny (Welsh) accent.

When he is left alone, Pistol turns serious; we learn that his wife, the hostess, has died of venereal disease (presumably syphilis) and that Pistol no longer has a home. He decides to become a pimp and a thief back in England.

SUMMARY: ACT V, SCENE II
At the palace of the king of France, King Henry has come to meet with Charles VI and his queen, Isabel. The goal of the meeting is to negotiate a lasting peace between France and England. Despite his military victory, King Henry will allow Charles to retain his throne. However, Henry has a list of demands, the first of which is that he get to marry his distant cousin, Princess Catherine of France. That way, Henry and his heirs will inherit France as well as England.

The others discreetly retire from the room, leaving Henry and Catherine alone together, with Catherine's maid, Alice, to help translate. In a comic scene, Henry courts Catherine, trying to persuade her to marry him. Understanding the gist of his flood of English words and few French ones, Catherine eventually agrees, pointing out that the decision is actually up to her father, "de roi mon père [of the king my father]" (V.ii.229).

The rest of the noblemen come back in, and Henry and the Duke of Burgundy trade some manly innuendoes about what Catherine will be like in bed. Everyone signs the treaties that will make Henry and his sons heirs to the throne of France after the king of France dies.

SUMMARY: ACT V, EPILOGUE
The Chorus appears for the last time to deliver the Epilogue. This very brief speech mentions the birth of Catherine and Henry's son, King Henry VI of England, who went on to lose France and bring

England into war. With a final plea for the audience's tolerance of the play, the Chorus brings the play to a close.

———————————————

ANALYSIS: ACT V, PROLOGUE, SCENES I–II, AND EPILOGUE
In Act V, scene i, Pistol, Gower, and Fluellen's final scene, the patriotic urgency that unites men of disparate nations in battle dissipates, and cultural conflict between the British allies again returns as Fluellen and Pistol insult each other. Fluellen's tormenting of Pistol with a leek provides comic relief and contrasts with Henry's treatment of the various characters—Scrope, Nim, and Bardolph—who have gotten on his bad side. Whereas Henry subjects those who run against him to death, Fluellen humiliates Pistol with a ludicrous but ultimately harmless punishment. Fluellen gives Pistol money to make up for his bruised head, demonstrating his compassion.

Pistol's revelation of the news of his wife's death adds an unexpected note of pathos to the end of the scene. It reminds us of the earlier deaths of Bardolph, Nim, and the boy, who was probably murdered with the other pages during the battle. The reminder of mortality darkens the play's conclusion and adds a note of realism to Shakespeare's presentation of his commoners. Even these comic characters must endure horrible tragedy. For a poor man like Pistol, an accident of fate can result in a terrible debasement—Pistol will now be forced to act as a pimp and thief merely in order to survive.

Act V, scene ii—the courtship scene between Henry and Catherine—is intended to close the play on a light note, but the scene contains some unsettling elements. Henry awkwardly makes courtship speeches, posing himself as an unpolished warrior. Henry has given far too many brilliant orations during the play for the audience to believe that he is no good at speaking. Henry's discomfort, or his lack of desire to woo Catherine, stems from the fact that Henry's manners are immaterial to his chances of success. Catherine is being used as a political pawn and barely understands the language her suitor speaks. As she points out when Henry asks her if she will "have" him, the decision her father's to make (V.ii.228–229).

Henry's kind treatment of his future wife and his show of seeking Catherine's consent to the marriage are undoubtedly meant to reassure Catherine and the audience that he will accept his role as a husband with the same commitment and faith with which he has accepted the role of king. Yet the suggestive sexual remarks that Burgundy and Henry trade after the French noblemen reenter are unsettling. Burgundy's reference to the "naked blind boy" of love, who will invade Catherine's maidenly virginity, alludes to the god Cupid but is also a phallic reference (V.ii.275). The references to Catherine's "naked seeing self" (V.ii.275) and to the "eyes" of maidens (V.ii.306) play on the Renaissance euphemism that substitutes "eye" for "vagina." The play, which throughout has examined the relationship between the noble and the common, concludes by juxtaposing mannered discussions of a marriage between high nobility and the earthy raunchiness of sex jokes.

The Epilogue, like Pistol's news from home, strikes an unexpectedly somber note: it reminds us that Henry and Catherine's son did not, in fact, do what they had hoped by uniting the two kingdoms. Henry V, though the ideal king, was not influential in a historical sense—he looks to overturn history, but instead history overturns him. As always, the Chorus points out the difference between a play about a brief period in English history, within which Henry V is a highly successful protagonist of potentially dubious moral character, and the full scope of that history, a context within which Henry proved largely ineffective.

SUMMARY & ANALYSIS

Important Quotations Explained

1. And tell the pleasant Prince this mock of his
    Hath turned his balls to gunstones, and his soul
    Shall stand sore chargèd for the wasteful vengeance
    That shall fly from them—for many a thousand widows
    Shall this his mock mock out of their dear husbands,
    Mock mothers from their sons, mock castles down;
    . . .
    But this lies all within the will of God,
    To whom I do appeal, and in whose name
    Tell you the Dauphin I am coming on
    To venge me as I may, and to put forth
    My rightful hand in a well-hallowed cause.
    (I.ii.281–293)

This passage is part of Henry's response to the messenger who delivers the crate of tennis balls that the Dauphin offers as a mocking reminder of Henry's irresponsible and wayward youth. With an icy, menacing wrath, Henry turns the Dauphin's jest on its head, threatening the messenger with a promise to treat the fields of France like a tennis court and play a game for the Dauphin's father's crown.

In his repeated insistence that the Dauphin's jest will be responsible for the terrible carnage that he will bring to France (the Dauphin will "[m]ock mothers from their sons"), Henry indulges in an early instance of casting responsibility for his actions away from himself and onto his enemies. By claiming to come to France in the name of God and by telling the Dauphin that he, the Dauphin, is responsible for the consequences, Henry presents himself as an unappeasable, unstoppable force his enemies must submit to rather than struggle against. Henry may seem arrogant, but he makes himself appear humble by appealing to God rather than to his own power. This speech thus becomes an early blueprint for almost all of Henry's future self-characterizations: he claims that his enemies' wickedness is to blame for the violence brought by his own army, then depicts himself as an instrument of God whose desire to further God's will leaves him no choice as to how to behave.

2.   Then imitate the action of the tiger.
     Stiffen the sinews, summon up the blood,
     Disguise fair nature with hard-favoured rage.
     Then lend the eye a terrible aspect,
     . . .
     Now set the teeth and stretch the nostril wide,
     Hold hard the breath, and bend up every spirit
     To his full height. On, on, you noblest English,
     Whose blood is fet from fathers of war-proof,
     Fathers that like so many Alexanders
     Have in these parts from morn till even fought,
     And sheathed their swords for lack of argument.
     Dishonour not your mothers; now attest
     That those whom you called fathers did beget you.
     Be copy now to men of grosser blood,
     And teach them how to war. And you, good yeomen,
     Whose limbs were made in England, show us here
     The mettle of your pasture. . . .
          (III.i.6–27)

This passage is from Henry's famous "Once more unto the breach, dear friends" speech, which ends with the battle cry, "God for Harry! England, and St. George!" Rallying his men to charge once more into the fray at the Battle of Harfleur (the "breach" refers to the hole in the town wall created by the bombardment of Henry's cannons), Henry employs two separate strategies for psychological motivation, each of which uses its own language and rhetoric. First, Henry attempts to tap into a primal instinct toward violence within his men, hoping to rouse them into a killing frenzy. To this end, he compares the expressions he desires his men to wear to the features of an angry tiger. He describes in great detail the savage features of tigers, urging his men toward a mindless fury represented by snarling teeth and flared nostrils. The vivid imagery of Henry's speech indicates his own experience with the savage passion of battle, as he commands his men to "[b]e copy now to men of grosser blood"—that is, to act as barbarians.

At the same time, however, Henry employs a second strategy whereby he inspires his men with a nationalistic patriotism, urging them to do honor to their country and prove that they are worthy of being called English. This sense of a shared national creed is somewhat more sophisticated than the urging to primal violence, and

Henry turns away from the blunt physical description in the early part of his speech to a more complex rhetoric that combines historical reference ("so many Alexanders"), a sentimental appeal to family pride ("[d]ishonour not your mothers"), and reminders of birthplace ("you, good yeomen, / Whose limbs were made in England"). At the end of his speech, Henry attaches St. George, the patron saint of England, to his legendary battle cry, providing his men with a treasured and familiar symbol of the patriotic ideals he espouses in his rally cry.

3.   'Tis not the balm, the sceptre, and the ball,
        The sword, the mace, the crown imperial,
        The intertissued robe of gold and pearl,
        The farcèd title running fore the king,
        The throne he sits on, nor the tide of pomp
        That beats upon the high shore of this world—
        No, not all these, thrice-gorgeous ceremony,
        Not all these, laid in bed majestical,
        Can sleep so soundly as the wretched slave
        Who with a body filled and vacant mind
        Gets him to rest, crammed with distressful bread;
        . . .
        And but for ceremony such a wretch,
        Winding up days with toil and nights with sleep,
        Had the forehand and vantage of a king.
        The slave, a member of the country's peace,
        Enjoys it, but in gross brain little wots
        What watch the King keeps to maintain the peace,
        Whose hours the peasant best advantages.
          (IV.i.242–266)

QUOTATIONS

This soliloquy by Henry is extremely important to the play because it gives us our only glimpse into Henry's psyche that is not compromised by his need to appear kingly in front of others. Sitting alone in his camp, disguised as a commoner, Henry reveals the crushing responsibilities he feels on his shoulders, with every man of England laying his soul, debts, wives, children, and sin on the king's head. Henry describes the lonely isolation of power, which is combined with the need to be eternally vigilant ("What infinite heartsease / Must kings neglect that private men enjoy?" [IV.i.218–219]). The only consolation Henry can see in being king lies in pomp and "ceremony"—Henry's word for the opulent show of royalty, with its rich clothes, parades, traditions, and self-aggrandizement. To Henry, ceremony is essentially empty, no more than a "tide of pomp" beating on a shore. Henry says that he would trade all that ceremony for the peaceful sleep of the slave, who has no greater concerns in his head than his stomach and who has no idea "[w]hat watch the King keeps to maintain the peace."

Henry's speech is somewhat self-pitying; after all, it is doubtful that a slave would find his life as easy as Henry seems to think. But Henry's willingness to envy a slave at all is rare for a monarch. Most kings are completely devoted to maintaining, solidifying, and increasing their power; for a king to abandon all his power would represent a complete failure of his intentions and desires. Even other kings who are conscious of the weight of responsibility they carry would shy away from such a statement. Henry V's father, Henry IV, for instance, complains at length in 2 Henry IV about the pressures besetting "the head that wears a crown," but it never occurs to him that his lot is less desirable than that of a slave (2 Henry IV, III.i.31).

Henry V's statements show his remarkable ability to look beyond the ingrained and commonplace value judgments of his society, entertain an independent perspective, and place himself imaginatively in the shoes of his subjects. Henry also shows how little pleasure he takes in his own power. He is motivated by a sense of responsibility to his subjects, a responsibility that he takes very seriously and that requires him to place his own personal feelings a distant second. He is unable even to express his sorrow at his condition to anyone else; only when he is alone can he relax enough to allow himself to feel his own regret. If Henry is self-pitying in this speech, it is in part because there is no one else to pity him.

QUOTATIONS

4.   If we are marked to die, we are enough
To do our country loss; and if to live,
The fewer men, the greater share of honour.
God's will, I pray thee wish not one man more.
By Jove, I am not covetous for gold,
. . .
But if it be a sin to covet honour
I am the most offending soul alive.
No, faith, my coz, wish not a man from England.
God's peace, I would not lose so great an honour
As one man more methinks would share from me
For the best hope I have. O do not wish one more.
Rather proclaim it presently through my host
That he which hath no stomach to this fight,
Let him depart. His passport shall be made
And crowns for convoy put into his purse.
We would not die in that man's company
That fears his fellowship to die with us.
            (IV.iii.20–39)

This quotation is from Henry's St. Crispin's Day speech, the rallying oratory he delivers to the English army just before the Battle of Agincourt. Presumably, the power of this speech assists his soldiers in routing a French force that outnumbers them five to one. Henry's opening lines, in which he explains why he does not wish for more men to fight with him, indicate his ability to give abstract moral concepts such as honor a tangibility and urgency that motivate his men far more powerfully than the repetition of platitudes about the glory of war would. Henry portrays the amount of honor to be won in the battle as a fixed amount that will be divided equally among all the victors; if there were more men present, then there would be less honor for each man to gain in victory. Henry's claim to favor a small army is centered on his stated desire for himself and his men to win as much honor as possible in the battle.

Henry's startling reversal of the normal conventions of battle make this idea effective. In most battles, the leader wishes for as large an army as possible in order to achieve an easier victory, but Henry claims to desire a small, outnumbered army to win a larger share of honor. In most battles, soldiers are compelled to fight and deserters are killed, but Henry backs up his claim to desire a small army by offering to let any man who does not desire to fight with him leave. Henry thus gives each of his soldiers the freedom to make the choice to fight with him; in doing so, he wins a measure of loyalty and devotion that he could not have commanded through force.

This speech is an example of Henry using his rhetorical skill to achieve the effect he needs—he does not really desire a small and outnumbered army, but he has a small and outnumbered army, and it is more effective to make his soldiers think that he is in the position he desires than to show them how difficult his position really is. Henry uses his ability to see things from unique perspectives to arrive at a surprising logic regarding honor and glory, then he uses his skill with words to make that logic stir his men to great deeds.

5.   I think it is e'en Macedon where Alexander is porn. I tell you, captain, if you look in the maps of the world I warrant you sall find, in the comparisons between Macedon and Monmouth, that the situations, look you, is both alike. There is a river in Macedon, and there is also moreover a river at Monmouth. . . . If you mark Alexander's life well, Harry of Monmouth's life is come after it indifferent well. For there is figures in all things. Alexander, God knows, and you know, in his rages and his furies and his wraths and his cholers and his moods and his displeasures and his indignations, and also being a little intoxicates in his prains, did in his ales and his angers, look you, kill his best friend Cleitus —
            (IV.vii.18–32)

Fluellen delivers this speech to Gower after Henry commands in the previous scene that the English soldiers kill all their French prisoners. Fluellen compares Henry to Alexander the Great, whom he initially calls "Alexander the Pig," meaning "Alexander the Big" (IV.vii.10). Fluellen bases his comparison upon the ridiculous fact that there is a river in the town where Henry was born and a river in the town where Alexander was born.

In addition to being amusing, the speech is important because of its somewhat ominous ending. Fluellen notes that Alexander killed his best friend, a crime of which the audience might also accuse Henry, who indirectly or directly causes the deaths of Falstaff, Scrope, and Bardolph. Shakespeare thus uses Fluellen's humor, in a moment of comic relief, to probe some of the moral anxiety lurking beneath his heroic portrait of Henry. Fluellen's comparison of

QUOTATIONS

Henry to Alexander is both amusing and highly flattering to Henry. But, by unintentionally making the darker connection that both men killed friends, Fluellen emphasizes one of the play's problem areas—namely, that running parallel to the qualities of leadership and justice in the minds of great kings is often a troubling capacity for violence and rage.

KEY FACTS

FULL TITLE
The Life of King Henry the Fifth

AUTHOR
William Shakespeare

TYPE OF WORK
Play

GENRE
History play

LANGUAGE
English

TIME AND PLACE WRITTEN
Probably 1599, London

DATE OF FIRST PUBLICATION
1600 (in quarto), 1623 (in folio)

TONE
Though there are moments of comedy, the overall tone of the play is elevated and serious, celebrating the intense personal charisma of Henry and the bloody military conflict between England and France.

SETTING (TIME)
Around 1414–1415

SETTINGS (PLACE)
London, at the royal palace and the Boar's Head Tavern; various locales in France, including the battlefields of Harfleur and Agincourt and Charles VI's court

PROTAGONIST
Henry V

MAJOR CONFLICT
Henry leads an English army to invade and conquer France. The outcome of this war will prove whether or not Henry has put aside his wild youth and become an effective ruler, and whether

he has the moral authority of a legitimate king—in other words, whether or not God is on his side.

RISING ACTION

Using Canterbury's explanation of Salic law as justification, Henry lays claim to France, but the French mock Henry's kingship and authority by sending him tennis balls as a token of his idle youth. Infuriated, Henry launches an invasion of France, putting his political aims above his personal ties and therefore showing no favoritism or leniency to his former friends.

CLIMAX

Before the Battle of Agincourt, in Act IV, Henry's delivers his impassioned St. Crispin's Day speech, emphasizing his unity with his subjects and his total commitment to the glory of England and the justice of his cause.

FALLING ACTION

The English victory at Agincourt is so lopsided that it seems like an act of God, making Henry one of the most famous and successful kings in English history. Henry is betrothed to Catherine and becomes heir of the French throne.

THEMES

The ruthlessness of the good king; the diversity of the English

MOTIFS

Male interaction; parallels between rulers and commoners; war imagery

SYMBOLS

The tun of tennis balls; characters as cultural types

FORESHADOWING

Henry's grim comments to the French ambassador about the havoc he will wreak in France foreshadow the English slaughter of the French at Agincourt.

KEY FACTS

STUDY QUESTIONS & ESSAY TOPICS

STUDY QUESTIONS

1. *What kind of a king is King Henry V? Is he a good king or merely a successful one?*

The qualities that make Henry universally admired include his bravery, his eloquence, his ability to appear regal or humble depending on the demands of the situation, and his willingness to step down from his position and talk with the common soldiers, as he does the night before the Battle of Agincourt. His less admirable qualities include his insistence on disowning his responsibility for other people's deaths and his heartlessness toward his former friends.

Whichever qualities we find most striking in Henry, it is important to note that in order to be effective, it is essential that Henry appear to be good. Henry's claim to the English throne is weak, since his father was a usurper, and for Henry to appear to be a legitimate king he has to seem like he has God on his side. Thus, for instance, he makes sure that the Archbishop of Canterbury publicly presents the arguments supporting Henry's legal claim to the French throne, even though the arguments are logically tortured, and even though the audience already knows that it cannot trust the archbishop.

Shakespeare provides us with plenty of clues that Henry is self-consciously performing the part of the good king, but he doesn't necessarily give us the sense that Henry is in fact bad. *Henry V* explores the idea that the qualities that make one a great king are not necessarily morally admirable ones—what makes a good king is not what makes a good person. Henry is willing to kill his former friends coldly and slaughter thousands of French people in the heat of battle to satisfy the demands of his throne; he must put his personal feelings second to the requirements of rulership and achieve the result he desires at any cost. Henry's act of placing responsibility for the war on others helps him to achieve his goals, as it burdens others with the moral pressure of stopping the war. This behavior may make Henry seem unlikable, but it also makes him a great leader and leads directly to the triumph at Agincourt in Act IV. Ultimately, the answer to the question may be that there are no good kings—just effective ones.

2.   *Henry V spends a lot of time simply giving speeches to others (to the French ambassador, before the town of Harfleur, and before Agincourt, for example). What effect do Henry's speeches have, and how are they important in the play?*

King Henry speaks a great deal in this play, as he understands the power of his words to elicit action. Sometimes his speeches are meant to stir soldiers' morale, as with the speech at the Battle of Harfleur in Act III, scene i, and before the Battle of Agincourt in Act IV, scene iii. Other times they are meant to intimidate, as when he speaks to the French ambassadors in Act I, scene ii or the governor of Harfleur in Act III, scene iii. Even when he is talking to his soldiers in disguise, as in Act IV, scene i, or courting Catherine in Act V, scene ii, Henry seldom gets interrupted and is usually able to sway the mind of the person to whom he is talking. Henry's side always wins in battle or argument, partly because Henry uses his charisma as an effective tool: for Henry, the act of speech, or rhetoric, is a vital weapon of both persuasion and war.

3.   *Women are almost absent from the play, allowing male-to-male relationships to dominate. What do you think of the male bonding, or the structures of friendship and enmity between men, in the play? Which characters have these relationships and which do not? How does King Henry participate in these relationships?*

Oddly enough, King Henry, the character around whom everyone else in the play revolves, spends much of his time alone—even when he is surrounded by a crowd. He is often surrounded by other people, but seldom talks to anyone alone or outside of formal war business. One exception is his interlude in disguise, in Act IV, scene i, in which he talks face-to-face with various soldiers, only to come away with a still stronger sense of the special position of a king.

In comparison to the sense of fellowship among Pistol, Nim, Bardolph, and the boy, or the friendship between Fluellen and Gower,

Henry doesn't seem to have any close friends. Falstaff, once a close friend, dies rejected in Act II, scene iii, and Henry has Scrope killed in Act II, scene ii, just before Scrope can attempt to assassinate him. It even seems dubious that Henry will find companionship with his future wife: Catherine, who barely speaks English, is marrying him for political reasons. King Henry exists in the strange isolation of power, a condition he touches on in his monologue the night before the Battle of Agincourt.

SUGGESTED ESSAY TOPICS

1. *Some contemporary critics are uneasy with Henry V because they feel it glorifies war and imperialism. They note that when the play was produced during the World War II era, it was easily turned into patriotic propaganda. Do you agree with their assessment? Does the play present a realistic picture of war?*

2. *How does Shakespeare use individual characters to present a broad panorama of the various peoples and cultures that were part of Britain during Henry's reign? What are some of these cultures, and how does Shakespeare's evocation of them relate to the Chorus's first speech before Act I?*

3. *Throughout the play Shakespeare employs a number of recurring metaphors to describe and characterize war. What are some of these metaphors? What do they have in common? How might they help the audience to picture a massive battle on a small stage?*

4. *How are marriage, families, and parenting treated in the play? How do they relate to the political realm?*

QUESTIONS & ESSAYS

Review & Resources

Quiz

1. Which of his friends does Henry execute for plotting to assassinate him?

    A.   Scrope
    B.   Falstaff
    C.   Bardolph
    D.   Randall

2. Where does Henry make his "Once more unto the breach, dear friends" speech?

    A.   Agincourt
    B.   Paris
    C.   Harfleur
    D.   London

3. Approximately how many French soldiers are killed at Agincourt?

    A.   150
    B.   10,000
    C.   30
    D.   4,500

4. Approximately how many English soldiers are killed at Agincourt?

    A.   50
    B.   10,000
    C.   100,000
    D.   30

5. From whom did Henry's father take the English crown?

    A. Richard II
    B. Richard III
    C. Edward IV
    D. Henry IV

6. Whom does Henry agree to marry as part of his treaty with France?

    A. Alice
    B. Michelle
    C. Courtney
    D. Catherine

7. Where does Henry make his "St. Crispin's Day" speech?

    A. Harfleur
    B. Agincourt
    C. Paris
    D. Warwickshire

8. In what year was Henry V probably first performed?

    A. 1560
    B. 1617
    C. 1618
    D. 1599

9. Who gives Henry tennis balls?

    A. The Dauphin
    B. The king of France
    C. Westmorland
    D. Exeter

10. Which of his friends does Henry execute for looting a French town?

    A. Exeter
    B. Chubb
    C. Bardolph
    D. Ancient Pistol

11. Which character is Welsh?

    A. The Dauphin

    B. Fluellen

    C. Nim

    D. Ancient Pistol

12. What action prompts Henry to kill the French prisoners?

    A. The murder of Alice

    B. The murder of Westmorland

    C. The murder of the English prisoners

    D. The murder of the English pages

13. What breaks Falstaff's heart?

    A. Henry's rejection of him

    B. His failure to defeat Owain Glyndwr

    C. His failure to seduce Mistress Quickly

    D. His failure to seduce Catherine

14. Who gives Henry a glove?

    A. Gower

    B. Warwick

    C. Williams

    D. Mistress Quickly

15. What is the Dauphin's attitude toward the English troops?

    A. Wary respect

    B. Mocking contempt

    C. Lighthearted camaraderie

    D. Open fear

16. Who is the king of France?

    A. Louis IX

    B. Henri IV

    C. Philip II

    D. Charles VI

17. Of what disease does Mistress Quickly die?

   A.   Cancer
   B.   Venereal disease
   C.   Heart disease
   D.   Alcoholism

18. What does Pistol plan to do at the end of the play?

   A.   Become a full-time soldier
   B.   Run Mistress Quickly's tavern
   C.   Become a pimp and thief
   D.   Become an actor

19. What does the Chorus do at the beginning and end of the play?

   A.   Point out the play's shortcomings
   B.   Boast about the play
   C.   Joke about the play
   D.   Lie about the play

20. What name will Henry's son take?

   A.   Richard III
   B.   Philip III
   C.   Edward I
   D.   Henry VI

21. Who tries to teach Catherine English?

   A.   The queen of France
   B.   The king of France
   C.   Henry
   D.   Alice

22. To whom does Henry threaten that his troops will rape women and murder children?

   A.   The mayor of Agincourt
   B.   The governor of Harfleur
   C.   The king of France
   D.   The minister of defense

23. Where does Henry make his speech about the tennis balls?

A. Harfleur
B. Agincourt
C. England
D. Reisa

24. Who was Henry's closest friend before he became king?

A. Falstaff
B. The boy
C. Gower
D. Bardolph

25. Who is married to the hostess?

A. Nim
B. Bardolph
C. Falstaff
D. Pistol

ANSWER KEY:
1: A; 2: C; 3: B; 4: D; 5: A; 6: D; 7: B; 8: D; 9: A; 10: C; 11: B; 12: D; 13: A; 14: C; 15: B; 16: D; 17: B; 18: C; 19: A; 20: D; 21: D; 22: B; 23: C; 24: A; 25: D

SUGGESTIONS FOR FURTHER READING

GREENBLATT, STEPHEN. *Shakespearean Negotiations: The Circulation of Social Energy in Renaissance England.* Berkeley and Los Angeles: University of California Press, 1988.

HARRISS, G. L. *Henry V: The Practice of Kingship.* New York: Oxford University Press, 1985.

LOEHLIN, JAMES N. *Henry V.* New York: St. Martin's Press, 1997.

ORNSTEIN, ROBERT. *A Kingdom for a Stage: The Achievement of Shakespeare's History Plays.* Cambridge, Massachusetts: Harvard University Press, 1972.

SEWARD, DESMOND. *Henry V as Warlord.* London: Sidgwick & Jackson, 1987.

TAYLOR, GARY. *Three Studies in the Text of Henry V.* Oxford: Clarendon Press, 1979.

SparkNotes™ Literature Guides